AFGHANISTAN	INDIA
AUSTRIA	IRAN
BAHRAIN	IRAQ
BERMUDA	IRELAND
BRAZIL	ISRAEL
CANADA	JAPAN
CHINA	KAZAKHSTAN
COSTA RICA	KUWAIT
CROATIA	MEXICO
CUBA	NEW ZEALAND
EGYPT	NORTH KOREA
ENGLAND	PAKISTAN
ETHIOPIA	RUSSIA
REPUBLIC OF GEORGIA	SAUDI ARABIA
GERMANY	SCOTLAND
GHANA	SOUTH KOREA
ICELAND	UKRAINE

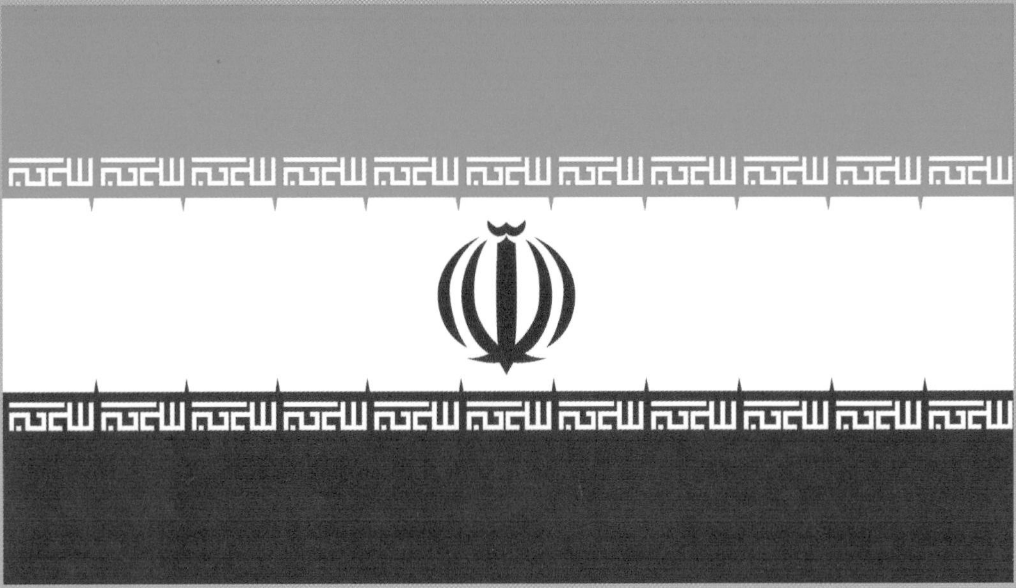

Iran

Masoud Kheirabadi
Portland State University

Series Consulting Editor
Charles F. Gritzner
South Dakota State University

CHELSEA HOUSE
PUBLISHERS
A Haights Cross Communications Company

Philadelphia

Frontispiece: Flag of Iran

Cover: The shrine of Shah Nematullha Vali, Mahan, Iran

CHELSEA HOUSE PUBLISHERS

VP, NEW PRODUCT DEVELOPMENT Sally Cheney
DIRECTOR OF PRODUCTION Kim Shinners
CREATIVE MANAGER Takeshi Takahashi
MANUFACTURING MANAGER Diann Grasse

Staff for IRAN

EXECUTIVE EDITOR Lee Marcott
PRODUCTION EDITOR Jaimie Winkler
PICTURE RESEARCHER 21st Century Publishing and Communications, Inc.
SERIES DESIGNER Takeshi Takahashi
LAYOUT 21st Century Publishing and Communications, Inc.
COVER DESIGNER Keith Trego
©2003 by Chelsea House Publishers, a subsidiary of Haights Cross Communications.
All rights reserved. Printed and bound in the United States of America.

A Haights Cross Communications Company

http://www.chelseahouse.com

First Printing

1 3 5 7 9 8 6 4 2

Library of Congress Cataloging-in-Publication Data

Kheirabadi, Masoud, 1951–
    Iran / Masoud Kheirabadi.
        p. cm.—(Modern world nations)
Includes index.
Contents: Introduction—Natural environment—Early history—Steps toward modern
Iran—People and culture—Government and politics in the Islamic Republic of Iran.
    ISBN 0-7910-7234-7 HC   0-7910-7502-8 PB
    1. Iran—Juvenile literature. [1. Iran.] I. Title. II. Series.
DS254.75 .K49 2002
955—dc21

                                                                    2002015901

Table of Contents

MODERN WORLD NATIONS

Iran

The shrine of Shah Nematullha Vali stands in front of mountains in Mahan, Iran. The Persian civilization was once among the most powerful in the world. Today, modern Iran reflects much of that rich cultural heritage in its art, architecture, music, and worship.

Introducing Iran

O nce a great world civilization, Iran still is one of the most fascinating nations of the modern world. It is also one of the world's most misunderstood countries. The political upheaval following the 1979 revolution created an image of Iran throughout the Western world, particularly in the United States, characterized by religious fanaticism, terrorism, and anti-Americanism. This image, though partially accurate, by no means represents the true nature of Iran and Iranians. As a matter of fact, up to the time of the revolution, Iran was a close friend of the United States. American presidents and officials frequently visited Iran and spent their vacations there. American advisers and consultants were seen all over the country, advising the government, the military, and industrial and other private enterprises.

Due to its breathtaking natural beauty and its rich cultural heritage, Iran was also a popular tourist destination for Americans and other tourists from different parts of the world. The country's physical beauty and cultural and historical sites still attract a large number of international tourists. The appealing warm waters of the Caspian Sea, the lush green forests of northern Iran, the majestic snow-capped summits of the Elburz Mountains, and the esoteric marshes and deserts of the central Iranian plateau provide Iran with one of the world's most diverse natural landscapes.

Iran's unique physical geography has made it a land of four seasons, where at any chosen time, a visitor can feel all four seasons by moving throughout the country. In northwestern Iran, people can take refuge from the chilly winds of the winter or ski on the snow-covered mountain slopes. At the same time, in the warm waters of the Persian Gulf in southern Iran, others can swim and water-ski to cool off from the heat of the day. The barren desert lands of central Iran also offer a sharp contrast to the dense forests covering much of northern Iran.

Iran is located at a "crossroads of civilizations." This historical factor, combined with its central location within the Middle East, gives the country considerable geopolitical importance. Historically, its central location has made possible regular contact between Iranians and neighboring cultures. Its rich natural resources have attracted many invading armies that have sought to control the nation during various periods of Iran's extensive history. The discovery of fossil fuels (petroleum, natural gas, coal) at the beginning of the twentieth century also brought first the British and later the Americans to Iran.

Iran is the only country that has access to two of the world's richest deposits of oil and natural gas—the Persian Gulf and Caspian Sea basin. Iran currently holds 9 to 10 percent of the world's total petroleum reserves and is among the largest producers and exporters of oil in the world. Iran also contains the second largest amount of natural gas deposits in the world,

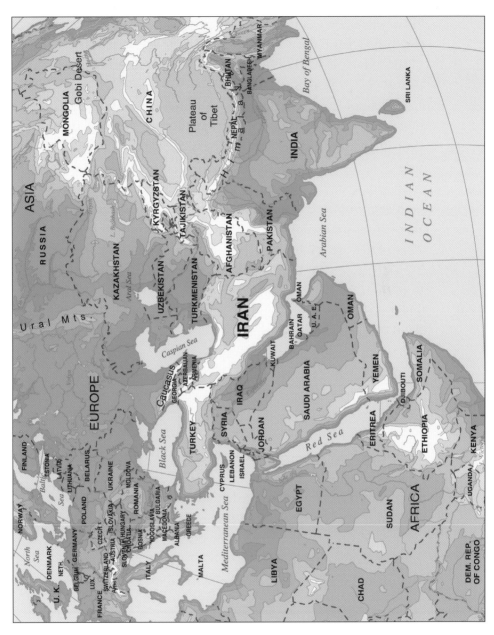

Located along ancient East–West trade routes, and home to vast natural resources of its own, Iran has long held a position of importance. The discovery of abundant fossil fuels in the early twentieth century made Iran an important trading partner for industrialized nations such as Britain and the United States. Iran currently holds just under ten percent of the world's oil.

after Russia. It is estimated that the country owns 15 percent of the world's natural gas. Fossil fuels have become the lifeblood of the industrial world, and Iran is a major contributor due to its vast energy resources.

Oil is not, however, Iran's only contribution to the world. In over 2,500 years of cultural and written history, its people have contributed to the development of global civilization in many ways. Iran has enriched world civilization in the areas of religion, science, art, literature, and politics. Iran provided the world with the prophet Zoroaster, who lived sometime during the seventh or sixth century B.C., and who was founder of the Zoroastrian religion, long before Jesus and Mohammed. Zoroastrianism was the first religion that introduced humanity to religious concepts such as angels, heaven, and hell, concepts which were later borrowed by Christianity. The origin of the word "paradise" comes from the Old Persian language. Later leaders of various Persian empires promoted Zoroaster's teachings, which declared that salvation comes through following the principle of "Good Deeds, Good Words, and Good Thoughts."

Iran also gave the world its first major empire. The Persian Empire, as it was known, predated the Greek Empire that was established by Alexander the Great. At its peak under Darius the Great, the empire stretched from the Indus Valley to the Nile Valley, and northwestward to the Danube River. Cyrus the Great, who founded the empire, liberated the Jews from many years of living in captivity when he defeated the Babylonian Empire to the west in 539 B.C. The Bible, in the Book of Isaiah, refers to Cyrus the Great as the liberator of the Jews. Many Jews who chose to remain in Persian territories are ancestors of the current Iranian Jewish population.

Iran is a land of linguistic, ethnic, and religious diversity. Even though Persian is the official language of modern Iran, other languages and dialects are spoken throughout the country. In addition to being multilingual, Iran is also ethnically diverse. Although Persians form the majority of the population, other groups residing in Iran include Turks, Arabs, Kurds, and Baluchis. Due to a long history of coexistence among these different ethnic groups, modern Iranians are of mixed blood and one can not easily distinguish the ethnicity of a particular individual by appearance alone.

It is not uncommon for a traveler to notice churches, synagogues, and Zoroastrian temples while driving in Tehran and some other Iranian cities. Although several religions are practiced today, most Iranians are Muslims.

Islam was introduced in Iran by an invading Arab army during the seventh century A.D. Soon after its introduction, however, Islam became a popular religion among Iranians. Many converted to the new faith and embraced the ideals of Islam. The simplicity, the inherent social justice, and the egalitarianism (equality) of Islam attracted many Iranians who were dissatisfied with the former stratified social system sanctified by corrupt religious leaders.

During the sixteenth century, the Safavid dynasty made the Shiite branch of Islam Iran's official religion, and Iran is now the largest Shiite Muslim country in the world. Gathering under the banner of Shiism, the country became united and was able to resist the expansionist tendencies of the emerging Turkish Ottoman Empire to the west. However, during the history of Shiism in Iran, Shiite clerics never controlled the national government until the emergence of the Islamic Republic of Iran in 1979.

Standing over 18,000 feet (5,671 meters) above sea level, Mount Damavand with its snow-capped volcanic cone is among the most picturesque mountains of the world.

2

The Natural Environment

GEOGRAPHICAL SETTING AND BORDERS

Extending between 25 and 40 degrees north latitude and 44 and 63 degrees east longitude, Iran covers an area about twice the size of California, Oregon, and Washington combined. With an area of some 636,296 square miles (1,648,000 square kilometers), it is also three times the size of France.

Situated in the heart of the Middle East in southwest Asia, Iran is a bridge linking Asia and Europe. To the north, Iran shares borders with three newly independent republics: Armenia, Azerbaijan, and Turkmenistan. Prior to their independence the former Soviet Union controlled all three. To the north, Iran also borders the Caspian Sea, the world's largest landlocked body of water. Due to its being landlocked, the Caspian Sea is officially considered a lake rather than a sea; however, due to its substantially large size, historically it has been referred to as a sea. To the south, Iran borders the Persian Gulf and the Gulf of Oman. It shares its eastern border with Afghanistan and Pakistan, its western border with Turkey and Iraq.

At their border, Iran and Iraq share a major body of water formed by the joining of major rivers that pour into the Persian Gulf. The Tigris and Euphrates rivers flowing in Iraq join the Karun River flowing in Iran to form the strategically significant body of water called Shatt-al Arab (Arabian River) by Iraqis and Arvand Rud (River Arvand) by Iranians. Due to its periodic meandering, the stream has been a source of boundary disputes between the two countries. One of the major objectives of the Iraqi government's invasion of Iran in September 1980 was the annexation of this strategic and economically important body of water.

TOPOGRAPHY AND EARTHQUAKES

As mentioned, Iran is located between two major depressions, the Caspian Sea to the north and the Persian Gulf to the south. A series of mountains rising steeply from these depressions, along with other isolated mountain chains, form a high outer rim that encloses the interior basin. This configuration provides Iran with an overall bowl-shaped topography that characterizes the country's general physical appearance. The interior basin is known as the Iranian Plateau. According to geologists, the plateau is an ancient former seabed that took its present shape during the Quaternary period about 200,000 years ago. It was formed and shaped by the uplifting and folding effects of three giant plates pressing against each other. The interacting plates are the Arabian Plate, the Eurasian Plate, and the Indian Plate. The continuous process of squeezing and pressing resulted in a considerable folding at the edges, and some folding in the interior, which eventually formed Iran's present mountain ranges.

The continuing geologic process of uplifting and folding is also responsible for earthquakes—subterranean shifts in the earth that take place near the numerous fault zones formed by the movement of the plates. About 90 percent of Iran falls within an active seismic (earthquake-prone) zone. Most of the country is subject to the tremors and the devastation that they can cause. On June 22, 2002, a major earthquake hit the northwestern region of Iran, causing significant damage and casualties to small mountain towns and villages in the area. The earthquake, with a force of 6.4 on the Richter Scale, occurred at 7:28 A.M. local time and was felt as far away as Tehran approximately 180 miles east of the epicenter. The death toll was 261 and the number of injured exceeded 1,300 people. In addition, over 25,000 people were left homeless. Many villages were totally destroyed and many others lost their water supply as a result of this earthquake.

A much more devastating earthquake occurred earlier, on June 21, 1990, in northern Iran. It caused 50,000 deaths, 100,000 injuries, and left 500,000 homeless. Other major earthquakes during recent decades have claimed the lives of many Iranian people. For example, a 1997 earthquake in eastern Iran with a magnitude of 7.1 on the Richter Scale killed 2,000 and destroyed 200 villages. Another quake, measuring 7.7, occurred in 1978 in the eastern province of Khorasan. It killed 25,000 people and completely destroyed the ancient city of Tabas along with a large number of villages. The cheaply built adobe (mud-brick) buildings are the main reason for the vast destruction and high death tolls.

TOPOGRAPHY AND WATER

The peculiar topography of Iran, particularly the orientation of mountains, has resulted in the country's general aridity. With the exception of two strips in the northern and western sections of the country, Iran consists mainly of dry lands and barren mountains. The rugged Elburz Mountains, which stretch in a general northwest–southeast direction along the southern shores of the Caspian Sea, block the moist northerly winds coming from the Caspian Sea and result in an uneven distribution of precipitation over the plateau. By the same token, the Zagros Mountains, extending from the northwest to the southeast of Iran, stand in the way of rain-bearing westerly winds coming from the Mediterranean Sea. Therefore, while the windward mountain slopes receive a considerable amount of moisture, the downwind central basins of the plateau receive very little precipitation.

The Elburz range contains numerous peaks rising above 12,000 feet (3,658 meters). Northeast of Tehran, Iran's highest peak, snow-capped Mt. Damavand, reaches an elevation of 18,605 feet (5,671 meters). With its impressive symmetrical volcanic cone, Mt. Damavand is one of the world's most majestic and picturesque summits. The steep northern slopes of the Elburz Mountains fall sharply from over-10,000-foot (3,048-meter) summits to the Caspian shores which lie about 90 feet (27.5 meters) below sea level.

The amount of precipitation varies from more than 50 inches (127 centimeters) on the Caspian coast to less than 2 inches (5 centimeters) in the desert areas. The central plateau, consisting of closed basins with an average elevation of 300 feet (90 meters), forms the most arid region of Iran. The annual rainfall here is less than 4 inches (10 centimeters), and the relative humidity rarely exceeds 20 percent. The most significant basins within the central plateau are the two salt deserts known as Dasht-e Kavir and Dasht-e Lut (dasht means "open land" in Persian). These barren regions are among the world's most inhospitable deserts, with their whitish salt crust, hot summer days, cold winters, and black, muddy marshes.

Mountain barriers (to prevailing winds) have resulted in a stunning contrast between relatively green slopes facing the incoming moist air and the barren slopes on the opposite sides which form the parched "rain shadow" slopes. This contrast

Occupying an area about three times the size of France, Iran is situated on a "bridge" of land that links Europe with Asia. Iran is bordered by Turkey and Iraq to the east, Pakistan and Afghanistan to the west, and by three countries formerly part of the Soviet Union to the north.

shows clearly in the distribution and settlement of the population throughout the country.

WATER AND SETTLEMENTS

The availability of water has always played a major role in the distribution and intensity of human activity in Iran. Most settlements occur on the sides of the mountains with access to water. For example, eastward-moving air coming from the Mediterranean Sea carries enough moisture to support a significant population in the western regions of Iran, mainly along the western slopes of the Zagros Mountains. These incoming moist air currents provide a relatively steady supply of surface water for some intermountain basins where cities such as Tabriz, Hamadan, Kermanshah, Shiraz, and Esfahan are located. The availability of water also allows green pastures that support livestock grazing.

Several rivers originate at high elevations in the Zagros Mountains. These streams bring prosperity and physical attractiveness to the cities they irrigate. For example, the city of Esfahan (Isfahan), with its large area beyond the city, is irrigated by the Zayandeh-Rud (Life-Giving River), which provides a fascinating focal point for the city. Other rivers, such as the Karun, Karkheh, and Dez, originate from the highlands of the Zagros Mountains, irrigate the fertile plain of Khuzistan in the southwest region of the country, and pass through large cities such as Dezful, Shushtar, Ahwaz, and Abadan.

Similarly, moist northerly winds blowing from over the Caspian Sea come in contact with the high Elburz Mountains and cause enough precipitation to support a sizable population along the northern slopes of the range and on the coastal lowlands bordering the Caspian Sea. The two provinces of Mazanderan and Gillan, located along the lower northern slopes of the Elburz, are among the most densely populated provinces of Iran. Cities located to the south of the Elburz Mountains, on the central plateau, receive much less precipitation. Tehran, for example, is located at an elevation of about 5,000 feet (1,500 meters) at the southern base of the Elburz. The city, Iran's largest, cannot survive without the use of underground water.

The coastal lowlands receive a considerable amount of rainfall year-round and are the most suitable lands for crop production. These lowlands receive runoff from the northern slopes of the Elburz Mountains, from such large streams as the Safid-Rud, Haraz, Babol, Tejan, and Gorgan. Due to this availability of water, the area is the most suitable place for production of crops such as tea and rice—the main staple in the diet of the Iranian people. Among the cities located on these lowlands are Rasht (near the Safid-Rud), Sary (along the Tejan River), Babol (on the bank of the Babol River), and Gorgan (on the Gorgan River).

There is no permanent river on the central plateau. Streams that reach the central plateau have dry beds for much of the year. During the spring, when mountain snow begins to melt, rivers begin to flow into salt lakes. But during the hot summer, these rivers dry up, as do most of the salt lakes into which they flow. Lake Urumia (also known as Rezaiyeh) is the most important permanent salt lake. It is located in the northwestern province of Azerbaijan (though it has the same name, this region is separate from the independent republic of Azerbaijan, located north of Iran and which was part of the former Soviet Union). Because of its high salinity and mineral content, Lake Urumia cannot support fish or any other aquatic life. It is, however, a main tourist attraction due to its natural beauty and its reputation that its water is able to cure various skin problems.

QANATS

Many areas bordering the central deserts receive fewer than 8 inches (20 centimeters) of annual precipitation, which is inadequate for dry (nonirrigated) agriculture. However, a traveler to Iran would be surprised to see many Iranian cities located along these fringes. How do these cities meet their water needs? An answer was found in an ancient technological innovation known in Iran as the *qanat*.

Qanats are subterranean aqueducts. Rainwater falling on the uplands runs off the bedrock and partly seeps into the gravel and sands at the base of the mountains, gathering in underground reservoirs. Qanats collect this fresh groundwater and carry it by gravity flow through gently sloping underground aqueducts (tunnels) to faraway settlements. Because qanats are often the only source of water, the distribution of settlements in the desert margins of Iran is closely related to the distribution of the qanat systems.

Winds also play a major role in the absence of cities in Iran's central desert. Winds affecting central Iran often carry with them sand and dust, so they damage crops and livestock, cover roads and houses, and continually change the surface features of the land. For example, the *baad-e sad-o-bist roozeh* (Wind of 120 Days), which originates over the central deserts during summer days, is hot and violent, carrying abrasive sand particles. With a velocity that can reach 70 miles (110 kilometers) per hour, it blows toward the provinces of Sistan and Baluchistan, destroying plants and vegetation, stripping away the soil, and damaging buildings and livestock.

Although the physical geography of the Iranian Plateau has a significant impact on the location of Iranian cities, it alone does not account for the presence or absence of settlements. One cannot ignore cultural factors, such as major trade routes, military and strategic requirements, and religious and political considerations.

CLIMATE AND VEGETATION COVER

Iran has the most diverse climate of all Middle Eastern countries. It varies from subtropical in the south to subpolar at high elevations. During winter, a high-pressure belt develops over Siberia. Its clear, often bone-chilling weather moves west and south to reach the interior basin of the Iranian Plateau. In contrast to this cold Siberian air, the warm waters of the Persian Gulf, Caspian Sea, and Mediterranean help to develop low-pressure systems over these waters. When these conflicting pressure systems meet, the dynamics exist for local wind formation.

The northwest is the coldest region of Iran. It is known for its cold winters with heavy snows and subfreezing temperatures during December and January. Summers in this region, however, are dry and hot, with spring and fall being relatively mild and pleasant. The south, particularly near the Persian Gulf, is known for its unpleasant climate. It has very hot and humid summers, with temperatures that have reached 123°F (50.5°C) in Khuzestan province at the head of the Gulf. The high humidity, accompanied by the excessive heat in this region, makes the weather almost unbearable for people from other parts of the country who are not used to it. Due to these harsh climatic conditions, people from Tehran, for example, who are asked by their companies to work in this region receive higher salaries than their counterparts working in Tehran. Winters, however, are mild, and are the best time to visit this area.

The Persian Gulf area, with its scorching heat and energy-sapping humidity, stands in sharp contrast to the Caspian coastal region to the north. In the Caspian region, moist air from the sea mingles with dry air currents from the Elburz Mountains and creates a pleasant nighttime breeze. The appealing warm water of the sea, accompanied by the pleasantly cool climate and beautiful natural land-scape, has made the Caspian Sea coastal areas popular tourist destinations.

The Caspian Sea region also receives the country's greatest amount of precipitation. In the high mountain valleys, the annual precipitation reaches as much as 80 inches (203 centimeters). The amount of precipitation is also distributed evenly throughout the year in this area. In contrast, with the exception of the high mountain valleys of the Zagros and Caspian coastal plain, precipitation throughout the rest of the country is relatively scant, and usually falls from October through April. The annual average precipitation for the country as a whole is around 14 inches (36 centimeters).

Roughly speaking, only about 10 percent of Iran is forested. While there are lush forests covering the northern slopes of the Elburz Mountains, the rest of the country has few forested areas. For example, the central deserts of Iran receive only a few

The Caspian Sea is the largest landlocked body of water in the world, making it a giant lake. Unlike the remainder of the nation, the Caspian Sea region receives ample annual rainfall, and the sea's warm waters make it a popular destination for visitors.

inches of precipitation each year. The scant moisture does not allow soil formation or much vegetation growth. In the Caspian region, the most common vegetation patterns are thorny shrubs and ferns, and broad-leafed deciduous trees, usually oak, beech, linden, elm, walnut, and ash, as well as a few broad-leafed evergreens.

In the Zagros Mountains one finds semihumid oak forests, together with elm, maple, walnut, pear, and pistachio. In the ravines, one can find willow, poplar, and plane trees, as well as many species of creepers. In the semidry plateau, thin stands of juniper, almond, and wild fruit trees are found. Steppes are covered by grasses and thorny shrubs, while acacia and dwarf palms often grow in areas below 3,000 feet (914 meters). In oases one can see tamarisk, poplar, date palm, myrtle, oleander, acacia, willow, elm, plum, and mulberry trees, as well as vines. Reeds and grass provide good pasture in swamp areas.

CLIMATE AND THE CITY

As has been discussed, with the exception of the two narrow regions bordering the Caspian Sea and the western slopes of the Zagros Mountains, Iran is an arid country. It is characterized by shortage of water, higher evaporation than precipitation, low relative humidity, intense solar radiation during hot summer days, high daily and seasonal temperature ranges, torrential (but sporadic) spurts of precipitation, and damaging sand and dust storms. Through centuries of coping with these climatic conditions, Iranians learned to build their settlements in a way to minimize the impact of solar radiation and harmful and unpleasant winds, and to optimize shade, breeze, and water.

Traditional cities adopted a compact urban form that included narrow winding streets, buildings set close together, houses with courtyard ponds, covered bazaars, and wind-capturing towers. The compact city form minimizes the empty space that can become a source of heat during the day and cold at night. The narrow winding streets provide shade for the passersby and protect them from sand and dust-laden storms. The courtyard ponds provide the surrounding rooms with cool air through evaporation. Wind towers harness cool air to cool off the rooms below. The covered bazaar protects shoppers from rain and cold and allows cool air to circulate. (For more information about connections between the structure of Iranian cities and the arid climate, see Masoud Kheirabadi's book *Iranian Cities.*)

Built in 512 B.C., Persepolis was the center for ceremonies and worship during the ancient Achaemenid Empire, which lasted from 550–330 B.C. This great empire was established by Cyrus the Great. Later, under Darius the Great, the Empire stretched from India to the Nile River. Darius ordered the construction of a magnificent palace at Persepolis, which can still be seen in these ruins today.

3

Early History

THE LAND OF IRAN

W hat we call Iran today is part of a much greater geographical area that once was home to a great culture and civilization. Today, traces of Iranian culture can be seen outside modern Iranian borders in places such as Pakistan, Afghanistan, Central Asia, the Caucasus, eastern Turkey, Iraq, and the southern Persian Gulf coastal region. These are all areas that historically were part of the Persian Empire and therefore were influenced by Persian culture. Iranians tend to refer to the realm of Iranian cultural influence as "Iran Zamin," meaning, in the Persian language, "the Land of Iran."

The term "Iran" is a derivative of the word "Aryan" (the noble). Iranians were a branch of Aryan tribes who entered Iran from central Asia sometime during the second millennium B.C. and settled in the western and south-central parts of what is now modern Iran. While Aryans are believed to be the ancestors of modern Iranians, there were many other groups who lived in Iran before their arrival in the region. As a matter of fact, the history of the earliest sedentary cultures, based on existing archaeological sites, can be traced back some 18,000 years. And evidence suggests that humans occupied the region as long ago as 100,000 years.

IRAN OR PERSIA?

Today confusion exists among many Westerners on the proper use of the terms Iran, Iranian, Persia, and Persian. What are the differences in meaning? The terms Iran and Persia are used interchangeably, because both refer to the same land. Persia was what the Greeks referred to when they spoke of Iran. The origin of the term comes from the term "pars" or "parsa," the heart of the great Persian Empire where today's Iranian province of Pars or Fars is located. So, Persian simply means Parsi, or people of Persia.

Iranians, however, have always referred to their land as Iran and considered themselves to be Iranians. In 1935 the government officially registered the name of the country as Iran and demanded that international community call it as such. This way Iran can be remembered as the continuation of the Iran Zamin (the land of Iran) founded and expanded by the Iranian ancestors, the Aryans.

PRE-ISLAMIC HISTORY

Aryans were nomadic people in search of better land when they entered the Iranian plateau toward the end of the second millennium B.C. The reason for their migration may have been that they exhausted the natural resources, such as croplands and pastures, in their homeland. A group of these immigrants settled along the western slopes of the Zagros Mountains and set the foundation for an emerging empire known in the West as the Achaemenid Empire. Most of Iran's present-day nomads, still living on the slopes of these rugged mountains, are descendants of the original Aryans.

ACHAEMENID EMPIRE (550–330 B.C.)

The Achaemenid Empire, known also as the Persian Empire, became one of the greatest empires that the world had ever seen. It was established by Cyrus the Great, who defeated the powerful Babylonian Empire in 539 B.C. While in Babylon, Cyrus ordered the release of Jewish prisoners who had lived in captivity for many years. For this he became known as the "liberator of Jews," as is revealed in Jewish history and as is documented in the Book of Isaiah in the Old Testament. The empire that Cyrus created reached its peak during the reign of Darius the Great (541–486 B.C.). Under Darius, the empire stretched from the western borders of modern India to the valley of the Nile River and included numerous satellite kingdoms.

Darius is called "a great statesman" in the Bible. For the first time in history, he ordered the use of coins in trade. The use of gold and silver coinage later revolutionized economic exchange and world trade. Achaemenid rulers constructed substantial highway systems and pioneered advanced irrigation techniques. They also codified commercial laws, created a universal legal system, devised a universal system of weights and measures, and developed a reliable mail and postage system. Today's U.S. Postal Service motto (used also back in the days of the Pony Express) that "neither snow, rain, heat, nor gloom of night" will stop the mail from its delivery is modeled after a motto originated by the Achaemenids.

Building the necessary infrastructure (physical links such as roads) facilitated trade and communication throughout the satellite territories and paved the way for further expansion of the empire.

With trade came the diffusion of new ideas and culture. Some of the Persian words for typical items of trade became widely used throughout the empire. Later, some of these words entered the English language. Persian was the official language of the empire used for inscriptions and proclamations; however, the more commonly used language throughout the empire was Aramaic.

Art and architecture also flourished during the reign of the Achaemenids. As a result of their extensive contact with the far reaches of the empire, the kings employed skilled artisans and professionals from different religious and cultural groups to work on major projects, such as the Persepolis, the winter capital of the Archaemenid Empire. Today, the impressive remains of Persepolis, located north of the modern city of Shiraz in south-central Iran, testify to the magnificent glory of Iran's past.

The Achaemenid Empire fell to the emerging Greek empire of Alexander the Great. To humiliate his defeated rival, Alexander burned the beautiful city of Persepolis when he defeated the last king of the empire in 330 B.C. However, Alexander was soon taken by the richness of Iranian culture and found the fusion of Greek and Iranian culture a noble idea. He married Roxana (Roshanak), a Persian princess, and encouraged 10,000 of his soldiers to marry Iranian women. A mass wedding in the city of Susa, ordered by Alexander, displayed his desire to complete the union of the Greeks and Iranians.

SELEUCIDS AND PARTHIANS

After the sudden death of Alexander in 323 B.C., at the age of 32, one of his generals ruled over most of the former Persian Empire and established a dynasty known as the Seleucids. During the Seleucids, Hellenistic art, architecture, and urban planning began to diffuse into Iranian territories and Iranian culture was enriched by incorporation of Greek cultural traits.

In 247 B.C., however, Iranians revolted against the Greek Seleucids and established a dynasty known as Parthians. Parthians, who claimed ancestry from both Persians and Greeks, managed to retrieve a good portion of the former empire. They adapted an administrative system similar to that of the Achaemenids and used the Persian language and a form of writing called Pahlavi script as their official language.

In 224 A.D. the last king of the Parthian dynasty was overthrown by Ardeshir, a rival power who claimed descent from the Achaemenids. Ardeshir, the son of Sassan, then established the Sassanid dynasty that lasted for over 400 years.

SASSANIDS (224–642 A.D.)

Early Sassanid kings were capable rulers. They expanded their empire to the extent that it became roughly equal in area to that of the Achaemenids. The city of Ctesiphon (in present-day Iraq) was their capital. Their rulers adopted the title of Shahanshah, meaning the "the King of Kings" in Persian. Sassanids are known for improving the quality of life in cities, and for developments in agriculture and technology.

Under the Sassanids the administrative system became more centralized, the tax system was reformed, and the army was reorganized to tie the military more closely to the central government than to local lords. New towns were built and education and health care were improved. Scholars were encouraged to translate books from other languages into Pahlavi, the language of the empire. Many of these books, especially those brought from India, later became popular reading throughout the Islamic world.

The structure of society consisted of four major classes: priests, warriors, secretaries, and commoners. This stratified system gave privileges to princes, petty rulers, priests, and landlords, and deprived the artisans and the peasants. The system was sanctioned and supported by the Zoroastrian priests, who became immensely powerful in the court of Sassanid leaders.

In 224 A.D., Ardeshir overthrew the last king of the Parthian dynasty and established the Sassanid dynasty, which endured for 400 years. In this relief, Ardeshir is seen receiving his crown from the god Ahura Mazda.

Zoroastrianism became the empire's official religion.

At this time Iran's archenemies were the Byzantines (Eastern Romans), whose capital was Constantinople (present-day Istanbul, Turkey). Toward the end of the Sassanid Empire, too many wars with the Byzantines had exhausted and weakened both sides. During the last years of the dynasty, the empire was characterized by economic decline, heavy taxation, religious unrest, rigid social stratification, the increasing power of provincial landlords, and a rapid turnover of rulers. These problems facilitated the Arab takeover in the seventh century.

ISLAMIC PERIOD

During the seventh century A.D., an invading Arab Islamic army defeated the Sassanids and introduced Islam to Iran. Up to this point, most Iranians had been Zoroastrians, the official religion of the empire. Zoroastrian church leaders acted as the moral supporters of kings and their policies. In this way, kings legitimized their power through support of religious leaders.

The Islamic army, which already had defeated the mighty Byzantines at Damascus (Syria), defeated the weak and demoralized Sassanid army in 641 A.D. Iranian soldiers, mainly recruited from peasant families, did not see an urgent need to protect their homes against the Arabs. They had already heard about the egalitarian message of Islam and assumed that a government ruled under the Islamic principle of justice would be better than the morally corrupt government of recent Sassanid rulers.

Thus, soon after its introduction, Islam became a popular religion among Iranians. Many converted to the new religion and embraced its ideals. Its simplicity and message of social justice and egalitarianism (equality) attracted many Iranians who were dissatisfied with the socially stratified system of the Sassanid Empire promoted by corrupt religious leaders.

Another factor that speeded up the conversion process was the fact that Arab rulers provided tax relief to those converting to Islam. Islam soon began replacing the Zoroastrian religion in many Iranian cities. However, it took until the ninth century before the majority of Iranians had become Muslims, as practitioners of Islam are called.

The Arab conquerors, like other past invaders, soon

embraced many elements of Iranian culture and adopted some of the Sassanid administrative practices. Among them were the office of *vizier* ("minister" in the Persian language); the divan, a bureau for controlling state revenues and expenditures; and court ceremonial practices. Many Iranians served as administrators and ministers at the courts of Arab caliphs.

Islamic conquests under the Arab rulers brought many new territories under the control of the Arab caliphs, and Islam became the ideological blueprint of a vast Muslim empire that matched those of the Achaemenids and Sassanids. A high degree of tolerance for religious, ethnic, and cultural diversity created a very successful empire known for its achievements in art, science, and technology.

Iranian intellectuals played a major role in developing the Islamic civilization. They contributed to the development of many branches of Islamic learning such as theology, philosophy, literature, jurisprudence, medicine, science, history, and geography. Although Arabic was chosen to be the official language of the court in 696 A.D., Persian remained the spoken language throughout most of the Iranian cultural region. The Persian language, however, adopted the Arabic script and borrowed many Arab words during Arab rule.

As had happened to other rulers in the past, the Arabs gradually lost control over the vast Iranian territory. Several local dynasties with central Asian origins challenged the Arab rule, gaining control over different regions. There was also infighting among these groups, and some came to be more powerful than others. Among the more significant dynasties of this period were the Samanids (875–1005), Ghaznavids (962–1186), and Seljuks (1037–1220). The cultural and scientific achievements during the Seljuk reign were significant. Under the leadership of Nizam al-Mulk, the popular Iranian vizier, many schools, universities, and observatories were built. In one of these observatories, Omar Khayyam, the well-known poet and mathematician, conducted much of his experimentation leading to the creation of a new calendar. The Seljuk rule, however, came to an end when the Mongols invaded Iran.

MONGOL INVASION

The Mongol invasion left a bitter legacy throughout Iran. Genghis (Chingiz in Persian) Khan devastated whatever city he passed through and killed a large number of Iranian people between 1220 and 1258. Mongol soldiers even destroyed the qanat (subterranean aqueduct) systems and made food pro-duction difficult throughout the region.

In 1258, Mongols captured Baghdad, the capital of the dynasty of the Abbasids, and by killing the last caliph, ended Arab rule in the region. However, life improved during the later Mongol rulers. Under Ghazan Khan and his Iranian vizier, Rashid ad Din Fazlullah, the economy revived, taxes were lowered, irrigation projects were built or repaired, and international trade improved. Due to an increase in commerce with China and India, Iran was more exposed to the art and culture of these great nations. For example, the Chinese influence in Persian paintings made Chinese-style miniatures popular in Iran.

Tamerlane, another ruthless Mongol, emerged as a world power when he conquered Central Asia. Like Genghis Khan, he invaded Iran and destroyed many cities, including Shiraz and Esfahan. Tamerlane, however, had a soft side. Later during his reign he became a patron of art and promoted architects and poets. His successors also built many mosques and religious schools. The Mongol rule came to its end when the Safavid dynasty emerged as a major power.

SAFAVIDS (1501–1722)

Since the invasion of Iran by the Arab army in 641, the Safavids were the first true Iranian dynasty to rule the country. The Safavids came to power in 1501 when they captured the city of Tabriz (in the northwestern province of Azerbaijan) and made it their capital. From there, they expanded their rule over territories as extensive as those of the Sassanids.

The Safavids claimed to be direct descendents of the seventh Shiite Imam, Musa al-Kazim. They thus legitimized their power through their connection to the family of Mohammad, the Prophet of Islam. The Safavids declared Shiite Islam as the official religion of the state and used proselytizing, and when necessary, force, to convert the Iranian population to the Shiite sect (Shiism). The Safavids at first managed their government as a semitheocracy (a government strongly influenced by religion). Kings considered themselves spiritual as well as political leaders. However, during the reign of later kings such as Shah Abbas the Great (1587–1629), religion and state began to distance themselves from each other.

Kings established a strong fighting force known as *qizilbash*, whose members were chosen from mainly Turkish-speaking tribes. Their rivals were the mighty Ottomans to the west. The Ottoman Empire—the Turkish Muslim empire with its capital in present-day Istanbul—was expanding in all directions. It managed to capture Iraq from the Safavids and were fighting battles over the control of Azerbaijan and Caucasus. In 1639, the Safavids and Ottomans signed a peace treaty that established frontiers in both Iraq and Caucasus. Those borders are still in effect between Iran and her western neighboring states.

Shah Abbas changed the Safavid capital from Tabriz to Esfahan. He and his successors showed a great interest in making Esfahan a showcase of architecture and city planning. By building several magnificent mosques, religious schools, bazaars, and palaces, Shah Abbas wanted Esfahan to surpass the Ottoman capital of Istanbul in grandeur and beauty.

Besides being a true patron of art, Shah Abbas also promoted commerce. He worked closely with the British to

The great mausoleum of Uljaytu (died 1316 A.D.) in Sultaniyya is one of the architectural achievements of later Mongols. While the earlier Mongols who invaded Iran were very destructive, the later Mongols embraced Iranian civilization and culture and many became patrons of art and architecture.

expel the Portuguese from Bahrain and the island of Hormoz in the Persian Gulf. He encouraged European powers to do business with Iran. There was a great increase and improvement in the production of fine silks, carpets, cloths, and metal ware.

Safavid power, however, declined during the reign of its last two rulers due to corruption, rivalries among army officers, mismanagement of state revenues and land, excessive taxation, decline in trade, and the weakening of the military organization. In 1722, the last Safavid king submitted to an Afghan tribal leader who invaded Iran and captured Esfahan.

Afghan's rule over Iran was short-lived. In 1736, Nader Shah defeated the Afghan army and established the Afshar dynasty. A powerful military leader, Nader Shah also defeated the Ottomans in Georgia and Armenia and the Russians on the Caspian Sea coasts, and restored territories controlled by the Safavids. He also took his army to India and defeated Indian rulers and brought back many treasures. Nader Shah's rule was followed by a period of anarchy during which many groups competed for power. Karim Khan (1750–1779) succeeded in overcoming rivals and establishing the Zand dynasty. Karim Khan refused to accept the title of Shah, insisting that he was a servant of the people rather than a king. History remembers him most for his kind rule.

QAJARS (1795–1925)

The Qajars took over Iran after they defeated the last Zand ruler in 1794. They moved their capital from Esfahan to Tehran, a city that continues to serve as Iran's capital. After overcoming the challenges to their power from tribal chiefs, they brought a relative degree of unity, peace, and tranquility to Iran during their earlier years. Qajar rulers (Shahs) referred to themselves as the shadow of God on earth, and by gathering the Shiite religious leaders around them, they further legitimized their rule over their subjects. They were absolute rulers and appointed different princes as heads of the states and provinces and established a large bureaucracy.

But during the Qajar reign, the Iranian economy was suffering, the bureaucracy and army were in disorder, and the government was very corrupt. Some rulers tried to improve the country's overall condition; for example, they attempted to strengthen the administration by reforming the tax system and asserting more control over the overwhelming bureaucracy at different levels of the government. They promoted trade and industrialization. They established new technological schools and invited foreign instructors to share their knowledge with young Iranians. They even reduced the influence of the clergy, who opposed modernization processes.

The Qajars also established a European-style cabinet with administrative responsibilities and a consultative council of senior princes and officials. They opened the Karun River in Khuzestan to foreign trade and opened European-style banks. However, overwhelming corruption and a rising demand among the public for more freedom and the right to participate in government decisions led to the 1906 Constitutional Movement, which will be examined in more detail in the following chapter.

Iran is the world's only true theocracy—a country where political power rests in the hands of religious leaders. Here, Muslim clergymen at a shrine in Qum line up to vote in parliamentary elections.

4

Steps Toward Modern Iran

RELIGION AND POLITICS

Among the modern nations of the world, Iran is the only theocratic country—one in which absolute political power is in the hands of religious leaders. Although the governments of Saudi Arabia, Libya, and Pakistan are considered to be theocratic to some extent, none is comparable to Iran in this regard. The only country with greater religious influence on its government was Afghanistan during the Taliban regime in the 1990s. However, the September 11, 2001, terrorist attacks on the World Trade Center in New York City and the Pentagon in Washington, D.C., which was followed by the United States' invasion of Afghanistan, put an end to the Taliban regime.

Why is Iran a theocracy? Why are religion and politics so

intertwined there? Perhaps the answer lies in the nation's past history. Prior to the arrival of Islam in the seventh century A.D., during the Sassanid Empire, Zoroastrianism was the official religion of the country. Especially under the reign of the last Sassanid kings, religious leaders played a significant role in legitimizing the kings' rule. They were always seen working closely with the kings, supporting their national policies, eliminating rival religious groups, and in some cases imposing unjust social and economic laws.

When Islam was brought to Iran, the influence of religion in politics was actually increased in some ways. The fact that the Prophet Mohammad was both the spiritual leader of Islam and the political head of the Islamic community justified to Iranians the legitimacy of an Islamic state with a religious figure occupying the highest political office. Thus, throughout the Islamic history, religion and politics have been closely intertwined.

The role of Mohammad as both a politician and spiritual leader stands in sharp contrast to that of Jesus, who — at least based on what has been written about him — disliked politics and advised his followers to stick to their spiritual growth and let Romans to do the governing. This fundamental difference in the personality of these two religious leaders is a main reason for different approaches to the role religion plays in politics in modern Christian and Islamic countries. We should not ignore, however, the fact that the West has gone through historic events such as the Renaissance and French Revolution to reduce the power of the church. Similar events have not yet occurred in the Islamic world.

In Iran, religion and politics became more intertwined when sixteenth-century Safavid rulers announced that Shiite Islam would be the country's official religion. When Safavid rulers claimed to be descendents of Shiite Imams, whose heritage is traced to Prophet Mohammed, they in effect legitimized their power. The Safavids claimed Iran as a safe haven for persecuted Shiites in other lands and became the champions and voice of Shiism throughout the world. Dynasties that followed the Safavids, especially the Qajars, also employed the high Shiite leaders in their courts and wanted them to support and sanction their policies and behaviors.

WESTERN INTERVENTION IN IRANIAN AFFAIRS

Beginning with colonization, the West partially met its industrial needs by expanding control over Third World lands and resources. Soon after the European voyages of discovery, European powers were competing with one another all over the world for domination of weaker nations and exploitation of their raw materials; Iran was no exception. By the nineteenth century, Iran, due to its resources and vital strategic location in the Middle East, became a pawn in a geopolitical game between the competing British and Russian empires. Being too corrupt and militarily weak, the Qajar rulers could not withstand the territorial aggression of these two superpowers.

The Russians long had sought to gain access to the warm waters of the Persian Gulf. They believed that by controlling Iran and Afghanistan they could achieve that goal. However, the powerful British had the Indian subcontinent under their control and did not allow the Russian ambitions to materialize. Qajars kings, under pressure, had to concede territory to both the Russians and British. In 1812, Russia claimed the Caucasus territories, including Armenia, Georgia, and Azerbaijan, under the Treaty of Gulistan. And with the Treaty of Turkmanchay in 1828, Russia also annexed Central Asian lands from Iran. In 1857, Britain also forced Iran to give up its rights over the City of Herat and other territories in present Afghanistan. These two powers, especially the British, constantly interfered in Iran's internal affairs and often used existing ethnic and tribal rivalries to their advantage.

The discovery of oil in Iran and its first successful exploitation by the British in 1908 made Iran an even more attractive place to world powers. Britain controlled the Iranian oil industry until 1951, when it was nationalized by Musaddeq's government.

THE EARLY CLERIC VICTORIES

Iranians disliked being ruled by despotic Qajar monarchs who were supported by European powers and often acted against the country's national interests. There were always resistance movements against foreign domination, and against decisions made by kings that were not in the national interest. For example, in 1890, when a Qajar king, Nasseruddin Shah, gave a British company a complete monopoly over production and sale of tobacco, Iranians, led by religious leaders, protested the act. A religious leader, Mirza Shirazi, issued a religious decree calling for abstaining from and boycotting the use of tobacco by Muslim Iranians. The economic damage resulting from the boycott led to the cancellation of the contract. This major victory for the clergy against the autocratic kings became known as the "Tobacco Movement."

THE 1906 CONSTITUTIONAL MOVEMENT

By the end of the nineteenth century, Iranian intellectuals felt the need for a national constitution which would limit the power of the Qajar kings. People from all different walks of Iranian society, including the clergy, secular intellectuals, and merchants, supported this constitutional movement. When businessmen decided to close the bazaar, Mozaaffaru-din Shah felt the economic pressure and granted Iranians their first parliament. It was known as the National

Consultative Assembly, or Majlis-e Showray-e Melli. Iran thus became a constitutional monarchy, under which the monarch's power was limited and elected members of parliament made the important decisions. The Constitutional Movement is considered to be the beginning of Iranian modern history.

The Qajar leadership could not accept this loss of power, so the next king ordered the bombardment of the parliament and the arrest and execution of some parliamentary members. After this, the parliament faced uncertainty, as did the rest of the country under the remaining Qajar kings. During this period there were many mass revolts, some for democratization of the country and other by ethnic groups seeking political autonomy. The British and the Russians, in exchange for favors, supported the corrupt Qajar kings against the wishes of the Iranian population. These foreign powers did not take decisions made by the Iranian parliament seriously and often acted based on their own self-interests. For example, when the Iranian parliament announced Iran's neutrality during World War I, Russia and Britain ignored this national decision and sent their expeditionary forces into Iran.

REZA SHAH: THE FIRST PAHLAVI KING (1925–1941)

By the end of World War I, the Qajar dynasty that had ruled over Iran since the late eighteenth century was in disarray. It had failed economically and had lost support among Iranians. The time was ripe for a major change. In 1921, with the help of British officers, a self-made military man named Reza Khan orchestrated a coup that demolished the powers of the ruling Qajar king. After several years of consolidating his position as the country's strongman, Reza Khan crowned himself Reza Shah in 1925, the first king of the Pahlavi dynasty. (He chose Pahlavi, a pre-Islamic name, because it symbolically related him to the past glorious kings of Iran.)

Reza Shah's choice of regime was a constitutional monarchy over a republic, which many Iranian intellectuals wanted. Neighboring Turkey had just put an end to another despotic dynasty, the Ottomans, and replaced them with a republican regime, so it was natural for the people of Iran to want to replace its own despotic system with a republican one in which the people, rather than kings, would run the country. However, Iran was doomed to have another king in Reza Shah.

In a hot national debate over the merits of a constitutional monarchy versus a republican system, many leading clergy interestingly chose the monarchy. Reza Shah had made an agreement with the leading clerics that five Islamic jurists would be involved in government decision making to ensure that the government functioned within the Islamic context. He ignored the agreement, however, as soon as he took office.

THE MODERNIZATION PROCESS

Reza Shah was a strong nationalist who did whatever he thought necessary to lead Iran toward modernization. Like his counterpart Kemal Atatürk in Turkey, his ideal model for successful development was Europe. He considered Islamic traditions as impediments to Iran's path toward modernization. He was ignorant of the necessary criteria for effective development, and was too stubborn to listen to those who understood the rationale for European success. Thus, his path to modernization was merely a blind imitation of the West, or the Westernization of Iranian society. He failed to develop the country internally in a systematic way by building the necessary physical and human foundations for development. There was much to be done in the area of education, economic independence, technological advancement, and especially social justice. He often forced his way on the Iranian parliament and Iranian people without any regard for human rights.

After World War I, Iran's Qajat dynasty was in disarray. Economic instability made the time ripe for change. In 1925, with the help of British officers, an influential leader named Reza Khan crowned himself Reza Shah Pahlavi, choosing a pre-Islamic name that linked him to earlier Iranian kings.

However, one should not overlook some of the needed reforms orchestrated by Reza Shah. By secularizing the Iranian legal system, education, and bureaucracy, he curbed the influence of the clergy, who had dominated most aspects of Iranian society. He also centralized the Iranian administration system and created a disciplined army. He put down ethnic insurgencies and united the country. Among other improvements made during his rule were a modernized railroad system, establishment of the University of Tehran, and travel by Iranian students to Western countries for their college education. He also opened the National Bank of Iran, formed ministries of commerce and industry, and established the census law.

MODERNIZATION OR WESTERNIZATION?

Today Reza Shah is admired for preserving an Iranian sovereignty that was endangered by both internal and external threats. At the same time, his cruelty in dealing with the clergy and their traditional followers is cited as the primary reason for the direction taken by the Islamic Republic after its successful ascension to power in 1979. Impatient in his rush to secularize and westernize the country, Reza Shah banned the wearing of traditional Iranian and Islamic clothing in public. Women were told to cast off their traditional cover known as *chadur* and wear Western dress. Men were ordered to wear Western suits, ties, and brimmed hats. Even the clergy were forced to shed their cloaks and turbans by which they were identified as clerics. The police enforced these rules and violators were beaten and imprisoned.

In 1935, when some traditional followers of clerics in the holy city of Mashhad protested the imposition of these laws, Reza Shah ordered the bombing of a mosque inside which the protestors were gathered. In the eyes of the clergy and their followers, this action was considered to be an ultimate act of disrespect for Islamic ideals. Reza Shah became an enemy of Islam to be opposed.

During the early years of World War II, Iran declared her neutrality and Reza Shah saw no need participate in a European war. But as had happened during World War I, Western powers disregarded Iran's wish and the country was occupied by Russian and British troops. In 1941, under external pressure, Reza Shah abdicated in favor of his young son and prince, Mohammad Reza, who became the second Shah of the Pahlavi dynasty. Reza Shah was taken to Johannesburg, South Africa, where he died in exile.

MOHAMMAD REZA SHAH: THE SECOND PAHLAVI KING (1941–1979)

Twenty-one-year-old Mohammad Reza Shah had neither his father's charisma nor his will to rule Iran. He was inexperienced and very much at the mercy of his foreign backers. At the same time, the Iranian parliament, under external pressure, changed its position and declared war against Germany. The Allies occupied and used Iran as a route to supply German-occupied Russia with food and war equipment. At the end of the war, when Hitler's forces were defeated, the Allies called Iran "the Victory Bridge."

Foreign forces remained in Iran from 1941 to 1946. The occupation fueled a nationalist fervor for independence from European powers. After the withdrawal of foreign forces, Iran searched for a way to rid itself of European political and economic dominance and their puppet Iranian kings. One of the first acts geared toward independence was the nationalization of Iranian oil by the Iranian prime minister, Mohammad Musaddeq, in 1951. Musaddeq's bold stand against British imperialism made him popular in Iran. He was helped by a group of religious leaders, including Ayatollah Kashani, who was also a member of parliament at the time—evidence again of religious figures becoming involved in Iranian politics.

Reza Shah's son, Mohammad Reza Pahlavi, though lacking his father's charisma or political skill, became ruler of Iran in 1950 after the abdication of his father during World War II. Reza Pahlavi is shown here reading his inaugural speech on February 16, 1950. He would remain the shah until the Islamic Revolution forced him into exile in 1979.

THE MUSADDEQ CRISIS AND RETURN OF THE SHAH

British oil officials left Iran and issued a boycott against Iranian oil, a move that hurt Iran's economy. By 1953, the economy was suffering high unemployment and high inflation. The Shah, under pressure from the Iranian people, left Iran and Musaddeq officially became the country's leader. The British, however, convinced the United States to intervene and bring the Shah back to power. By this time World War II had significantly weakened the British, and the United States had become a world power. Soon after the war ended in 1945, the United States and the former Soviet Union were competing for world political, strategic, and ideological domination in a rivalry known as the Cold War.

To protect American oil interests in the region on one hand and contain the Soviet Communist expansion on the other, the U.S. Central Intelligence Agency (CIA) became directly involved in Iranian internal affairs. The CIA, British intelligence, and Iranian officers supporting the Shah orchestrated a coup that resulted in the overthrow of the government of Mussadeq and reestablished the deposed Shah's monarchy. To prevent further internal threats to the Shah's government, the CIA provided training to the Iranian secret police, known as SAVAK (*Sazmann-e Amniyat va Ittilaiat-e Keshvar*), meaning the Agency for Security and Information (affairs) of the country.

SAVAK's job was to guarantee the regime's security and stability. In pursuing this assignment, the agency soon became notorious for its brutality and lack of respect for human rights. Many political opponents speaking in favor of democracy and human rights were falsely labeled as communists, arrested, and often tortured or executed in prisons. American involvement in overthrowing Mussadeq's government, and later its unconditional support for the controversial Shah, gradually created a negative image of the United States government in the minds of Iranian intellectuals. America now had become the Shah's major ally and supporter in Iran.

Like his father, the Shah is credited for modernization reforms. Iran's infrastructure, public health, and educational institutions were expanded. Highways, roads, bridges, railroads, water and sewage projects, factories, schools, as well as universities and hospitals were built. In the early 1960s, under pressure from the administration of U.S. President John F. Kennedy, the Shah pioneered a series of reforms known as the "White Revolution" or the "Shah-People Revolution." The White Revolution included projects such as land reforms, public ownership of industries, nationalization of forests, voting rights for women, workers' profit sharing programs, and literacy and health corps educating and developing Iranian villages. These reforms, while looking good on paper, largely failed because of the rampant corruption of government agencies and officials. Some of these reforms, such as confiscating land from rich landowners and distributing it to peasants, and the emancipation of women, were opposed by certain religious leaders.

EXILING AYATOLLAH KHOMEINI

In 1963, Ayatollah Khomeini, a bold and popular Islamic religious leader, spoke out against the Shah's White Revolution, prompting his followers to pour into the streets and denounce the ongoing reforms. Khomeini was arrested and then released. Soon after his release, Khomeini again was criticizing the Shah's government for pushing legislation that granted U.S. military personnel immunity from local laws. The Shah, like his father, was not in the habit of involving religious leaders in Iranian politics. Clerical influence had been significantly reduced, and those who dared to oppose his policies were labeled as fanatics and were punished. Khomeini was rearrested and sent to live in exile.

Since legal opposition parties were not tolerated, those who opposed the Shah's government had to go underground and establish "guerrilla" (unofficial military) movements. During the 1970s, when the Shah seemed to be secure in his position, there were many different guerrilla groups fighting the government. Their ideologies ranged from communism to Islamic fundamentalism. Usually these opposition members, when identified and arrested, were labeled communists. As such, most were persecuted and some were executed. By being labeled communists, their elimination was supported by the U.S. government, which considered communism to be a threat to American interests during the Cold War.

"WESTOXIFICATION" OF IRANIAN SOCIETY

During Richard Nixon's presidency, the Shah and the U.S. government enjoyed a close relationship. Nixon, unlike Kennedy, was not critical of the Shah's human right abuses. In the Nixon administration's "Twin Pillar" policy for the Middle East, Iran was considered the military pillar and Saudi Arabia the financial pillar. The Shah fought for American interests in the Middle East and often publicly supported U.S. policies in the region. For example, through-out the Arab-Israeli wars, the Shah supported Israel.

Iran also financially benefited from the misfortune of Arab countries. In 1973, when Arab countries protested America's support for Israel during the war and refused to sell their oil, Iran increased production. With the sharp drop in regional oil production, prices increased fourfold, providing Iran with a huge increase in revenue.

Increased revenue, however, did not help the Iranian masses. The Shah's ambition to put Iran among the world's economic and military giants led to massive government spending. This included the purchase of the latest military equipment, mainly from the United States. Huge government spending encouraged by Iran's overnight prosperity began to strain the country's inadequate infrastructure, overheat the economy, create high inflation, and cause shortages of consumer goods. One of the major problems was a steep increase in the price of real estate in Tehran. Many low- and middle-income people could not afford soaring rental costs. At the same time, the government was bringing laborers and professionals from abroad, offering them free housing and high salaries.

The government-run television stations were also promoting Western culture and way of life by showing programs such as Western soap operas during prime time viewing hours. Many Muslim intellectuals found these programs distasteful for a traditional Muslim country. Many Iranians also believed the Shah's government was destroying the traditional Islamic way of life and recasting the country in an American image. A popular Iranian author called the process "Westoxification," meaning that the society was losing its customs, values, and spiritual principles because it was becoming "intoxicated" by Western (interpreted as "materialistic") values. Universities became the bastions of opposition and were raided by SAVAK and police forces on a regular basis.

With society in disarray, some intellectuals returned to traditional Islamic values. By 1978, the opposition to the Shah's regime had become widespread. Meanwhile, Khomeini had left his place of exile in Iraq and was living in France. From there he communicated with his followers through smuggled cassette tapes and political pamphlets.

THE SHAH'S DEPARTURE

In 1978 students demonstrated in the holy city of Qum, located south of Tehran. Police put down the demonstration, resulting in six deaths. Throughout the country, more demonstrations followed, and many more demonstrators were killed. Those killed were considered martyrs. Each additional fatality added more fuel to the fire of revolt, a flame that was burning out of control. Soon Iranians were asking for the Shah's removal. To please the Iranian population, the Shah, who was also suffering from cancer at the time, shuffled the membership of his cabinet, choosing individuals who were more popular with the masses. Although he appealed to the public with many promises, nothing seemed to work. Finally, on January 16, 1979, the

Shah and his family left Iran to live in exile. This was a sad occasion for a man who only several years earlier had had himself crowned as the successor of Cyrus the Great in a costly ceremony conducted before many official world dignitaries. His departure paved the way for the arrival of Khomeini and his Islamic Revolution, which will be discussed further in Chapter 6.

A man dances to celebrate the Persian New Year. Iran is home to many ethnic groups, each with their own dialect, customs, and traditions. Discrimination based on ethnicity is rare in Iran, and interethnic marriages are common.

5

People
and Culture

With a current population of about 70 million, Iran is one of the largest countries in the Middle East. It is also one of the most diverse Middle Eastern countries in terms of culture and ethnicity.

POPULATION TRENDS

During recent decades, Iran's population has been one of the fastest growing in the region, having doubled since the Iranian Revolution in 1979. During the 1980s there was a huge increase in the birthrate as a result of the new Islamic government's population policies (or, some suggest, the lack of policies). The new regime cancelled the Family Planning Program that was put in place in 1967 to educate families about contraceptives and to improve the status of women in the areas of divorce laws and employment. Clerics considered the program to be a product of Western influence and ordered health officials to stop distribution of contraceptives. Ayatollah Khomeini advocated higher birthrates, calling unborn Iranian children the future soldiers of Islam. Policies such as offering material rewards for larger families encouraged a steep increase in population growth. Between 1980 and 1988, when Iran and Iraq were fighting a pointless and destructive war, the annual population growth rate reached well over 3 percent.

A DEMOGRAPHIC SUCCESS STORY

By the late 1980s, Iran was suffering from a number of social and economic problems. Cities were overcrowded and polluted, unemployment was high, there were not enough schools for growing numbers of youth, and even paper and pencils were in short supply. The government began to reevaluate its population policies. In 1989, the national family planning program was revived. The government encouraged women to wait three to four years between pregnancies and for families to limit themselves to three children.

During the 1990s, the government began a bold campaign against overpopulation. The government-controlled news media began advertising the benefits of smaller families. Different institutions such as the Ministry of Education, Culture, and Higher Education and the Ministry of Health and Medical Education were asked to incorporate information on population, family planning, and mother and child health care in curriculum materials. Punitive measures such as restricting maternity leave benefits for mothers who have more than three children were implemented. Contraceptives and even sterilization became accessible from family planning clinics without cost to families. More than 15,000 of these mobile clinics were located throughout the country.

Unlike a decade earlier, clerics became actively involved in the national crusade for smaller families. They went so

In the 1990s, the Iranian government began a full-scale campaign against overpopulation. Here, women work in a condom factory. Contraceptives are distributed free of charge in Iran, in an attempt to encourage greater family planning and smaller families.

far as to encourage male and female sterilization along with other birth control means. The government even sponsored a condom factory in its attempt to make contraceptives more readily available. Perhaps the most effective policy was that which requires couples to take a class on family planning and use of modern contraceptives before receiving a marriage license. This was a somewhat innovative approach since it requires males as well as females to learn about contraception and family planning.

A combination of the foregoing factors, plus a dramatic increase in female literacy, caused a significant drop in population growth during 1990s. By 2001 the natural rate of increase dropped to 1.2 percent per year, reaching the level seen in developed countries. The birthrate was 18 per 1,000 and death rate 6 per 1,000 people during the year 2001. Iran's total fertility, rate—the average number of children born to a woman in her lifetime—plummeted from 6.6 (4.5 urban and 8.1 rural) in 1977 to 2.8 (2.2 urban and 3.5 rural) in 1996 and further to 2.0 (1.8 urban and 2.4 rural) in 2000. A rate of 2.1 is considered to be replacement level, so currently the population is no longer replacing itself. The extraordinary success of Iran in reducing her population growth in such a short period has made the country's population policy a significant model to be considered by other developing countries. (*See* Figure 5.1.)

DISTRIBUTION OF POPULATION

Iran's population distribution has been greatly influenced by a rapid pace of rural-to-urban migration. This trend started in the 1960s and shows no sign of slowing down. Today over 60 percent of Iranians live in cities, and rural areas continue losing population. (*See* Table 5.1 Population of Iran by Province.) One of the main reasons for this trend is a great gap in the standard of living that traditionally has existed between rural and urban areas. There has been considerable improvement in the lives of villagers, but city life, with its promise of entertainment, job opportunities, and excitement, sounds more attractive to rural youth than farming in remote villages. The fact that 65 percent of the Iranian population is under 25 years of age increases the likelihood of movement to urban life.

The Tehran metropolitan area remains the most attractive destination for immigrants from elsewhere in the country. More than 10 million people, or one of every six Iranians, live in Tehran Province. It has a population density of almost 1,400 people per square mile, while the average population density for the country is 94. This means the province is 15 times more densely populated than the country, on average.

The agriculturally fertile provinces of Gilan and Mazandran on the southern shores of the Caspian Sea are the next most

Figure 5.1 Total Fertility Rate by Province, Iran, 2000.
Source: Iranian Ministry of Health and Medical Education, UNICEF, and UNFPA, Demographic and Health Survey Iran 2000, *Preliminary Draft Report (2002).*

crowded Iranian provinces, with population densities of 412 and 283 people per square mile respectively. The central provinces of Semnan, Yazd, and Kerman have very low densities of 13, 26, and 29 respectively.

The city of Tehran, with a population of over 7 million, is Iran's largest city. Other cities with a population of over one million are Mashhad, Isfahan, Tabriz, Shiraz, and Karaj.

PROVINCE	POPULATION	AREA (km.²)	AREA (mi.²)	POP DENSITY PER SQ MILE	CAPITAL
Ardabil	1,168,011	17,881	6,904	169	Ardabil
Bushehr	743,675	23,168	8,945	83	Bushehr
Chahar Mahall and Bakhtiari	761,168	16,201	6,255	122	Shahr-e-Kord
East Azerbaijan	3,325,540	45,481	17,560	189	Tabriz
Esfahan	3,923,255	107,027	41,323	95	Esfahan
Fars	3,817,036	121,825	47,037	81	Shiraz
Gilan	2,241,896	14,106	5,446	412	Rasht
Golestan	1,426,288	20,893	8,067	177	Gorgan
Hamadan	1,677,957	19,547	7,547	222	Hamadan
Hormozgan	1,062,155	71,193	27,488	39	Bandar-e-Abbas
Ilam	487,886	20,150	7,780	63	Ilam
Kerman	2,004,328	181,714	70,160	29	Kerman
Kermanshahan	1,778,596	24,641	9,514	187	Kermanshah
Khorasan	6,047,661	302,966	116,976	52	Mashhad
Khuzestan	3,746,772	63,213	24,407	154	Ahvaz
Kohkiluyeh and uyerAhmadi	544,356	15,563	6,009	91	Yasuj
Kordestan	1,346,383	28,817	11,126	121	Sanandaj
Lorestan	1,584,434	28,392	10,962	145	Khorramabad
Markazi	1,228,812	29,406	11,354	108	Arak
Mazandaran	2,602,008	23,833	9,202	283	Sari
Qazvin	968,257	15,491	5,981	162	Qazvin
Qom	853,044	11,237	4,339	197	Qom
Semnan	501,447	96,816	37,381	13	Semnan
Sistan and Baluchestan	1,722,579	178,431	68,893	25	Zahedan
Tehran	10,343,965	19,196	7,412	1396	Tehran
West Azerbaijan	2,496,320	37,463	14,465	173	Orumiyeh
Yazd	750,769	73,467	28,366	26	Yazd
Zanjan	900,890	21,841	8,433	107	Zanjan
Total	**60,055,488**	**1,648,195**	**636,372**	**94**	

Table 5.1 Population of Iran by Province
Source: Iranian National Census

MANY DIFFERENT PEOPLES

Iran is one of the most ethnically diverse countries of the Middle East. Its location along the ancient Silk Route linking two major cultural hearths—China and the eastern Mediterranean—plus several thousand years of civilization, made it an attractive destination for immigrants. Throughout its long history, immigrants came both as invaders and as peaceful settlers. When they found themselves within the domain of Iranian culture, after a while they too adopted Iran as their home and contributed to further development of Iranian civilization.

Today's Iran is an ethnic and cultural mosaic. A visitor traveling within the country will see a variety of customs, clothing, music, art, food, and language. Physically, Iranians are a diverse people, ranging from light-skinned populations along the Caspian coast to dark-skinned populations along the Persian Gulf. Ethnically, the dominant group is Persian—people who trace their roots to early Aryan immigrants who established the first important Iranian empires. Persians form about 50 percent of the current Iranian population and are the most widely distributed people throughout the country. For most of Iran's political history, Persians have ruled the country.

Other ethnic groups include Azaris, Gilakis, Mazandaranis, Kurds, Arabs, Lurs, Balochs, and Turkomans. There is no social prestige associated with any particular ethnic group. Also, prejudice and discrimination based on ethnic origin is a rare phenomenon in Iran. Interethnic marriages are common. Due to a long history of coexistence, most modern Iranians are of mixed ancestry and their ethnicity is difficult if not impossible to recognize based on physical appearance. Tehran is the most ethnically diverse Iranian city.

Some ethnic groups have not yet settled in cities and continue to live a nomadic lifestyle. Their number is estimated to be about 1.5 million, most of whom are pastoral nomads. Some of the nomads, such as Bakhtiaris, Kurds, Lurs, Gilaks, and Baluchis, are descendants of original Aryan nomads who entered the Iranian Plateau during the second millennium B.C. and still live on the slopes of the Elburz and Zagros mountains. Other groups such as the Qashqais, Turkomans, and Afshars are descendents of Mongols and Turks who came later. Classic films (also available in video) such as *Grass* and *People of the Wind* have documented the electrifying transhumance (seasonal migrations) of Bakhtiari nomads in western Iran.

LANGUAGES

Travelers driving on the roads between Iranian provinces are surprised by the variety of languages and dialects they can detect listening to their car radios. They can shift from one station reading Persian poetry to another one playing Turkish songs, and then change again to another station broadcasting in Kurdish. Iran is quite unique among the world's nations in this respect. It is one of the few countries in which three linguistic families — Indo-European (Indo-Iranian), Altaic (Turkic), and Afro-Asiatic (Semitic)—are used by different groups, and occasionally even by the same people on different occasions!

Although numerous languages are spoken, the Indo-Iranian languages are the most widely used throughout the country. About two-thirds of the population speaks some type of Indo-Iranian language. The most important Indo-Iranian languages are Persian, Kurdish, Luri, Bakhtiari, Baluchi, Dari, Gilaki, Mazandarani, and Armenian. Persian is the official language of the country and the language of business and official communications. Different dialects of Kurdish are spoken among Iranian Kurds who live in western Iran, mainly in the provinces of Kurdistan and Kirmanshah. Luri and Bakhtiari are spoken by Lurs and Bakhtiaris who live on the slopes of the Zagros Mountains. Baluchi is spoken in the eastern provinces of Sistan and Baluchistan, and Dari is spoken in parts of Khorasan, especially areas near the border of Afghanistan. Gilaki and Mazandarani are the local dialects of people who occupy the provinces of Gilan and Mazandaran on the northern slopes of the Elburz Mountains. Armenian is the language of Iranian Armenians who live in Tehran and in northwestern parts of Iran.

Farsi (or *Parsi*) is the official linguistic term for Persian. It was introduced by the early Aryan immigrants. The name of the language was changed from Parsi to Farsi in the seventh century A.D. when the Arabs ruled Iran. Since the Arabs could not pronounce the letter "P"—the sound does not exist in the Arabic alphabet—all the "P" sounds in Persian words were converted to "F," a letter they could pronounce. Two centuries of Arab rule thus left its imprint on Iranian culture and Persian language. In addition to Parsi being called Farsi, today the Persian language is filled with Arabic terms that have been borrowed during many centuries of cultural contact.

Linguistic scholars recognize three forms of Persian: Old, Middle, and Modern. Old Persian was the language spoken throughout the Persian Achaemaenid Empire extending from the Mediterranean to the Indus River in western India. The famous cuneiform inscriptions of Darius are written in this language. During the Persian Sassanid Empire, Middle Persian or Pahlavi was used. This language, used until the ninth century A.D., was written in the Assyrian alphabet, as is displayed on some of the Sassanid rock carvings.

Modern Persian became dominant with the arrival of Arabs and Islam in the seventh century A.D. The alphabet was changed to Arabic with a number of additional characters to accommodate sounds that did not exist in the Arabic language. Although Modern Persian uses the Arabic alphabet, it is a totally different language than Arabic. Unlike Arabic, it does not have masculine and feminine words and it is easier to learn than Arabic.

Today's Persian is spoken with many dialects throughout the country. Each region has its own specific dialect and accent. For example, a person from Esfahan speaking his own dialect known as Esfahani is easily distinguished from a person from Mashhad who speaks with Mashhadi dialect. The most commonly used dialect is the dialect of Tehran, country's capital. Often the Tehrani dialogue is used in the media, including movies, national radio, and television.

Although Iran is the main Persian-speaking country, Persian is also spoken outside the current boundaries of Iran in

Islam is the dominant religion in Iran, and the country is dotted with shrines like this one. Shiite Muslims, although comprising only 15 percent of the world's Islamic population, are the dominant sect in Iran.

parts of Afghanistan, Tajikistan, and by Iranians in southern Persian Gulf countries. An examination of Persian vocabulary can help us to understand its Indo-European roots. Some of the English words with Persian origin are: cummerbund, shawl, pajama, khaki, kiosk, divan, lilac, jasmine, julep, jackal, caravan, checkmate, and bazaar.

RELIGION AND CULTURE

As mentioned in an earlier chapter, during the seventh century A.D., the defeat of the Sassanids by the invading Arab Islamic army brought the religion of Islam to Iran. Soon after its introduction, Islam became popular among Iranians and many converted to the new religion and embraced its ideals.

SHIITE ISLAM

Iranians, however, did not accept the religion of their invaders in its imported form. From the beginning there was a great interest in the Shiite sect of Islam in Iran. After the death of the Prophet Mohammad in 632, Islam was divided into the Sunni and Shiite branches. The difference between the two is not as much theological as it is political. Soon after the death of Mohammad, Muslims disagreed about the legitimacy of his successor. Most Muslims accepted the decision by the heads of powerful clans that Abu Bakr, Mohammad's close friend and father-in-law, should be the next leader. But another group of Muslims strongly believed that the succession should continue in the family line of Mohammad and therefore the next head should be his cousin and son-in-law, Ali. This group became known as the Shiite al-Ali, meaning the partisans of Ali. Through time, the word al-Ali was dropped from the end of the term.

Though today Shiites comprise only 15 percent of the world's more than one billion Muslims, in Iran Shiism is the main belief system. In fact, Iran is home to the world's largest Shiite population. During the sixteenth century, the Safavid dynasty made Shiism Iran's official religion, and by the mid-seventeenth century the majority of Iranians were Shiite (Shias.) Gathering under the banner of Shiism, the country became united and was able to resist the expansionist tendencies of the emerging Turkish Ottoman Empire to the west. However, Shiite clerics had never controlled the national government as they do now under the Islamic Republic of Iran.

FOUNDATIONS OF ISLAM

Muslims, like Christians and Jews, are monotheistic, believing in one God. The God of Islam is the same as the God of Abraham, Moses, and Jesus. It is called "Khoda" in Persian and "Allah" in Arabic. Although Muslims consider Islam a continuation of Judeo-Christianity, they do not accept the concept of the trinity.

Muslims also believe in prophets named in the Old Testament of the Bible. In fact, many Iranians name their children after biblical characters that are also mentioned in the holy book of Muslims, the *Qu'ran* (Koran). For example, Maryam (Mary) and Sarah are two of the most popular names for Iranian females. Among other popular names are Mosa (Moses), Isa (Jesus), Ebrahim (Abraham), Dawood (David), Suleyman (Solomon), Yusef (Joseph), and Yaqub (Jacob).

According to Muslims, Mohammad was chosen by God to be his last prophet in the line of Abraham, Moses, and Jesus. The Quran was revealed to Prophet Mohammad through the Angel Gabriel. The Qu'ran is believed to be the exact word of God and today there is only one Arabic version of the Quran, while there are numerous translations in different languages.

The Prophet Mohammad serves as the ideal man for every Muslim to emulate. Muslims also believe that human beings are responsible for their deeds and will be judged on Judgment Day. On that day there will be a resurrection of body and soul so everybody can face trial. If one's good deeds prevail, the eternal heaven awaits them, and if their bad deeds prevail, they will be inhabitants of hell. According to Muslims, God is compassionate and merciful. They believe that he has sent prophets to lead them along a straight path and that it is their religious duty to follow the path of God as it is explained in the Qu'ran and in the *Hadith*, books documenting prophetic sayings and deeds.

THE CONCEPT OF IMAMATE

A major Shiite belief that is not shared by Sunnis is the concept of imamate (the office of *Imam*, or Muslim religious leader). According to Shiites, after Mohammad's death, twelve of his descendents served as political as well as spiritual leaders of the Muslim community; thus, Iranian Shiites are known as Twelver Shiites. Like the prophet, these Shiite Imams were considered to be sinless and had the ability to interpret the inner mysteries of the Qu'ran and the *sharia*

(Islamic law). According to Shiites, the imamate started with Ali, Prophet Mohammad's cousin and son-in-law, and continued through his male offspring. According to Twelvers Shiites, the Twelfth Imam never died, but started a period of occultation by his physical disappearance in 939 A.D. It is believed that he is spiritually among his followers and that when God ordains, he will come back as Mahdi, or Messiah. Shiites' concept of Mahdi is similar to the concept of Jesus in Christianity. Mahdi, according to Twelver Shiites, is Lord of the Time, and devoted Shiites await his arrival; whenever his name is called, people rise as a sign of honoring his presence. His birthday is always a joyous occasion.

Iranian Muslims, like other Muslims throughout the world, believe in the Five Pillars of Islam. The first pillar is *Shahada,* or profession of faith that indicates oneness of God and Mohammad, God's last prophet. The second pillar is the ritual-ized daily prayers called *namaz* in Persian. The third pillar is *zakat,* or alms giving, which should be used to take care of the needy and the necessities of the Islamic community. The fourth pillar is fasting (*roozeh* in Persian) during the holy month of Ramadan, the month in which the Quran was revealed to Prophet Mohammad. The fifth pillar is *haj,* a pilgrimage to the city of Mecca in today's Saudi Arabia, where the holiest construction in Islam, the Ka`ba, or house of God, is located.

RELIGIOUS MINORITIES

While Shiites comprise 90 percent of the Iranian population, there are other religious groups living in Iran as well. About 9 percent are Sunni Muslims and 1 percent are Christians, Jews, Zoroastrians, and Bahais. Sunni Muslims are scattered around Iran, living mainly in border areas. Most Kurds, almost all Baluchis and Turkomans, and a small portion of Arabs are Sunni. Educated Shiites do not distinguish much between Shiites and Sunnis and consider Sunnis as fellow Muslims.

Most Christians are Armenians and Assyrians, groups

who were the original Iranian Christians. They are recognized as an official religious minority by the Islamic Republic and have their own representatives in Iranian parliament. Armenians are the largest group, with some 25,000 living mainly in Tehran, Esfahan, and Tabriz. They have maintained their own language, churches, and traditions and have blended well into larger Iranian society. Assyrians number between thirty and forty thousand and are mainly concentrated in northwestern Iran around Lake Urumia. There are also small numbers of Roman Catholics, Anglicans, and Protestants who were converted by Christian missionaries in Iran during the last two centuries.

Jewish history in Iran dates to the sixth century B.C. when Cyrus the Great released captive Jews. Many of today's Iranian Jews are descendents of those Jews who chose to remain in Iran. Like Christians, Jews are considered "people of the book" and are recognized as a legal religious minority by the current Iranian regime. They choose their own representatives to serve in the parliament. Currently, there are an estimated 30,000–40,000 Jews living in Iran.

Jews are mainly urban and live in Tehran, with smaller communities in Esfahan, Shiraz, Kashan, and Hamadan. Jews do not enjoy the same prosperity that they enjoyed under the Pahlavi regimes. This has resulted in an out-migration of many Iranian Jews to Israel and the United States. Political hostility between the Iranian and Israeli governments has been a reason for occasional mistreatment of Jews by the Islamic government.

Today there are still some 3,000 Zoroastrians in Iran, most of whom live in Tehran, Kerman, or Yazd. As an officially recognized religion, Zoroastrians have their own representatives in Iranian parliament.

Bahaisim is not recognized as an official religion; therefore, Bahai minority groups have not been treated well by the Shiite clergy who rule over Iran. They are a large minority of 350,000 mainly living in Tehran with small numbers scattered

After Cyrus the Great freed the Jews from the Babylonian Empire in the sixth century B.C., many Jews chose to remain in Iran. Although many Jews continue to live in Tehran and surrounding communities, recent political hostility between Iran and Israel has caused many to emigrate to Israel and to the United States. Here, an Iranian Jew prays in a synagogue.

elsewhere. Bahaism is an Iranian religion that originated in the 1840s as a religious reform movement within the Shiite Islam. Soon after its emergence, however, Bahais were considered heretics of Islam and were persecuted. During the Pahlavi regimes, Bahais were prosperous and free to proselytize (seek converts to) their faith. The current political regime has not allowed Bahais to proselytize, and many members of the faith have complained about being harassed by government officials.

In February 1979, Ayatollah Ruhollah Khomeini returned from exile and waved to a crowd of his supporters in Tehran. The rapid westernization of Iran under the Shahs had been viewed with hostility by many Iranian Muslim conservatives. As Mohammad Reza Pahlavi and his family departed the country in 1979, the exiled religious leader Ayatollah Khomeini returned home and built a coalition that established Iran as an Islamic Republic and solidified his leadership.

6

Government and Politics in Iran

LONGING FOR AN IDEAL GOVERNMENT

While Iranians were almost unanimous in opposition to the Shah's government, they seemed uncertain about the kind of government they actually wanted. Most people wanted a government that was politically independent from outside powers. They did not want a government that would promote the Western way of life at the expense of Iranian and Islamic values. They wanted a government that was democratic and that respected human rights. People also hoped for leadership that could manage the national economy more efficiently and create jobs and access to opportunities regardless of people's socioeconomic class. Most of all, they wanted a government that was not corrupt. Did the next government satisfy these legitimate demands? This is a question that has not yet been fully answered.

RETURN OF AYATOLLAH KHOMEINI

As has been discussed, many opposition groups fought against the Shah's regime. The best-organized of these groups, and those with greatest support of the Iranian masses, were the Islamic groups led by Khomeini. Four days after the Shah's departure, Khomeini ended his 14-year exile abroad, and in January 1979 he entered Iran and received an unprecedented welcome from the Iranian people. Journalist Peter Jennings of ABC News, reporting on Khomeini's return to Tehran, compared his role in Iran with that of Mao in China.

With his great confidence and charisma, Khomeini appealed to Iranians from all different walks of life. Soon after his return, he put together a coalition made of conservative clerics, secular leftists, nationalists, and moderate reformers, all of whom firmly believed in his sincerity and leadership skill.

Khomeini first had to confront the Shah's appointed prime minister, who was still running the country. Before his departure, the Shah had installed Shapur Bakhtiar, a popular senior politician, to this office. The armed forces remained loyal to Bakhtiar. Upon his arrival, Khomeini also appointed his own provisional prime minister, Mehdi Bazargan. Bazargan was a popular author and engineer with deep roots in the religious community. He also was an old colleague of Bakhtiar's from the National Front party. Iran now had two different governments, one of which would have to step down.

Bakhtiar tried in vain to convince skeptics that his reformed secular government was a better choice for Iran than Khomeini's religious government. But demonstrators wanted power to be transferred to Khomeini and his appointee, Bazargan. They still considered Bakhtiar the Shah's appointee; his survival would mean the continuation of a monarchy in Iran. The followers of Bakhtiar's regime were also greatly out-numbered by followers of Khomeini and Bazargan.

Some people worried that a military coup might save the

Shah's regime as it had in 1953 during Mosaddeq's era. This time, however, the wounds were too deep to cure and Iranians were too anxious for a new regime. When the Iranian armed forces declared their neutrality in conflicts between revolutionaries and the former regime, Bakhtiar had to step down from his post. Power was transferred to Khomeini and his revolutionaries.

THE ISLAMIC REPUBLIC

On April 1, 1979, a national referendum recognized the "Islamic Republic" as the legitimate government of Iran. The Islamic Republic, with its Islamic constitution, replaced the constitutional monarchy of the Pahlavi regimes. It is interesting to note that the Islamic Republic's constitution was mainly modeled after the French presidential parliamentary system. The key difference, however, was the insertion of a provision that granted the ultimate authority to a supreme religious leader, known as *vali-ye faqih*, meaning the ruling jurisprudent. The supreme spiritual leader, rather than the president or parliament, thus has the last word. Ayatollah Khomeini occupied this post until his death in 1989.

This revolution was unique because it ended some 2,500 years of on-and-off monarchy in Iran. Also, unlike the previous major revolutions, such as the French Revolution or the Russian Revolution, which took so many lives, this revolution was relatively bloodless. This revolution changed the path of Iran and Iranians both internally and externally. Today there are still debates concerning the need for revolution. Did it move the country forward on its path of modernization and development, or set it backward? Intellectuals both inside and outside the country are still debating questions such as these. What has become obvious is that the post-revolutionary Iranian government is far from being what so many Iranians hoped for and fought to gain. Many Iranians, however, still believe that the current government is a major improvement over that of the Shah.

Iranians can now elect their leaders, at least theoretically.

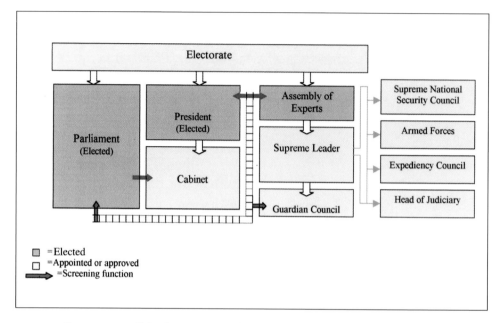

Figure 6.1 Political Structure of Islamic Republic of Iran

Due to a complicated system of filtering candidates on the basis of their ideological orientation, many qualified individuals are unable to run for government office. And even when they are elected by popular vote, they are powerless in the face of clerical domination of power. For example, President Khatami, president at the time of this book's publication, was twice elected by land-slide victories, and the elected members of the Iranian parliament are frustrated over their inability to implement reformist policies. Hard-line clergymen playing partisan politics and trying to preserve the status quo often block such reforms. Absolute power remains in the hands of the supreme leader and a power-ful network of clerics and other influential individuals who are not often elected by Iranian people.

IRAN'S POLITICAL STRUCTURE

According to the constitution of the Islamic Republic of Iran, absolute sovereignty belongs to God and the Islamic government is the trustee of this sovereignty. Since clerics are the most qualified interpreters of God's words as revealed in the Qu'ran and of the Prophet Mohammad's sayings and deeds collected in the books of Hadith, they therefore should run the government. In addition, according to the constitution, an Ayatollah (literally meaning the "Sign of God" on earth), who has mastered the Islamic law, should serve as the country's supreme head. This clearly makes the government a theocracy. However, there are also other elements within the system that are elements of a democracy (see Figure 6.1).

Democracy or Theocracy?

Today, Iran's political system is part democratic and part theocratic. The theocratic aspect often undermines the democratic processes, a fact that is the source of major complaint by contemporary Iranian reformists. Reformists seek changes in the system that will empower the president and parliament to implement their reformist policies. Although a majority of Iranians are Muslins who have great respect for the Islamic way of life, they do not appreciate the suffocating dominance of their country's affairs, including their private lives, by the clergy. They want more democracy and less theocracy in their government.

The Supreme Leader

What makes the system theocratic is the addition of two powerful positions—the office of the Supreme Leader and the Council of Guardian. At the top of the Iranian power pyramid is the Supreme Leader. He is the commander of the armed forces, head of the judiciary system and national radio and television, and leader of the clergy in the Council of Guardian (see following section). Some Iranians compare the role of the Supreme Leader with that of the Shah, who could do whatever he pleased without being answerable to anyone. The Supreme Leader is selected for life, and not by the people but by his like-minded clerics. And he is not answerable to the Iranian population. Ayatollah Khomeini occupied this position until his death in 1989. Since then, Ayatollah Khamenei has occupied the position.

The Guardian Council

The Guardian Council is another theocratic office of the government. A very powerful body, the council's primary task is to ensure that bills passed by the parliament conform to Islamic principles. Bills do not become laws until approved by the council. Between 1988 and 1992, the Guardian Council rejected about 40 percent of all bills passed by the parliament.

The council is composed of 12 members. Six members are theologians appointed by the Supreme Leader, and six are jurists nominated by the judiciary system (which includes mainly clerics) and approved by the parliament. This council also has to approve the candidacy of individuals running for government offices and can veto candidates for presidency, parliament, local councils, and the Assembly of Experts (see following section).

These twelve nonelected members of the Guardian Council routinely block decisions made by some 200 elected officials in the Iranian parliament. This situation is what many Iranians recognize as being a deviation from the path of democracy. They also resent the fact that many highly popular individuals with excellent qualifications are unable to become candidates for office simply because their views are unacceptable to religious hard-liners.

Assembly of Experts

The Assembly of Experts is, at least in theory, the most powerful cog in the mechanism of Iranian politics. In practice, however, this is not what has occurred during recent years. The assembly consists of over 90 clerics who supposedly appoint, oversee, and, if necessary, dismiss the Supreme Leader. However, the assembly recently has been criticized for its passivity and submissiveness to the Supreme Leader. Members of the assembly are elected directly by the electorate and serve for eight years. This is a theocratic body, but members are elected democratically.

Parliament

The Iranian parliament, known as *Majles*, is the most secular democratic body within the Iranian political structure. Begun in 1906, it also is the oldest democratic institution in the country. Members of parliament are elected by popular vote to four-year terms. Due to population increases since the 1979 revolution, the number of parliamentary seats has grown from 273 in 1980 to 293 in 2000. Like the Congress in the American political system, people of different provinces elect their representatives to the parliament. Recognized religious minorities such as Christians, Jews, and Zoroastrians also elect their representatives. In the past, the parliament was occasionally forced to close due to pressure from the kings. Thus, the new Iranian constitution ensures that the parliament cannot be closed for any reason and elections will be held under any circumstances.

Among parliament's most important functions are drafting legislation, passing international treaties, approving state of emergency declarations and loans, discussing and approving the annual budget, and, if necessary, impeaching and possibly removing the president and cabinet ministers.

Parliament vs. the Guardian Council

Constant challenges by the Guardian Council pose the greatest problem for the parliament. Unlike members of parliament, who are often secular and reformists, most members of the council are conservative clerics. This difference often results in reformist bills being blocked by the conservative council. Supposedly the council opposes bills that are in opposition to Islamic principles, but many of the bills they reject do not deviate from Islamic standards and ethics.

Due to this constant blocking of bills by the Guardian Council, a mediating office was established to serve as an intermediary between the parliament and the council. This Expediency Council faded away after Ayatollah Khomeini's death, but emerged again during the late 1990s to attempt resolving conflicts between the parliament and the council.

The Expediency Council

The Expediency Council consists of prominent religious, social, and political figures known for their capability in arbitrating conflicts. The council is a policy-making body with some legislative power. It also serves as an advisory body to the Supreme Leader.

In 2002, the former president Hojjatolislam Hashemi Rafsanjani heads the Expediency Council. Rafsanjani is considered to be the second most powerful Iranian political figure, after the Supreme Leader.

The President

Another elected office is that of president. Symbolically, at least, this office represents the most noticeable difference from the Shah's regime. In the past, Iranians were not able to elect important individuals such as presidents. At the beginning of the revolution, this office was occupied by secular individuals. During the most recent four terms, however, it has been held by clerics.

The president heads the executive branch of government. His primary job is to ensure the rule of law by implementing the nation's constitution. He is in charge of the day-to-day running of the country. As of 2002, Hojjatolislam Mohammad Khatami was serving his second term as president. Prior to Khatami, Hojjatolislam Hashemi Rafsanjani occupied the office for two terms. The president is elected for four years and can serve only two terms.

President vs. Supreme Leader

Khatami won the election by a landslide victory, having made promises to end the overwhelming governmental corruption, reform the economy, implement the rule of law, respect the human rights of individuals, stop the harassment of intellectuals and free-thinking people by government thugs, empower women, and relax the harassment of youth by the morality police. However, when he took office he had to face conservatives and their uncompromising views regarding reform and change. His proposed reforms have been restricted by conservative clerics of the legislative and judiciary branches, and by the absolute authority of the Supreme Leader. It is the Supreme Leader, rather than the president, who controls the armed forces and has the last word. In Third World countries with rudimentary democratic processes, whoever controls the armed forces usually controls the country.

The Cabinet

After his election, the president selects his cabinet ministers, who must be approved by the parliament before they can begin their duties. Also, since clerics are wary of the potential westernization of Iranian society, they constantly monitor the activities of ministers dealing with cultural and social issues. The cabinet consists of some 20 ministers and is chaired by the president or by the vice-president in his absence.

Supreme National Security Council

The Supreme National Security Council coordinates foreign policy, defense, and security issues. Their decision-making meetings are chaired by the president and usually involve representatives of concerned ministries and institutions. Due to the importance of the council's decisions, its ministers report directly to the Supreme Leader.

Armed Forces

The Supreme Leader also heads the country's armed forces, of which there are two branches: the regular force, which retains almost the same structure as the prerevolutionary military, and the Islamic Revolutionary Guard Corps (IRGC), which is a postrevolutionary force. The IRGC was initially put together to protect the revolutionary leaders and guard against anti-revolutionary threats. It was a counterbalance to the regular army, which was believed to be promonarchy.

In the beginning years of the revolution, the IRGC fought against rival groups such as the Islamic Marxist Mojahedin-e Khalq and the leftist Fedaiyan-e Khalq. It also put down ethnic insurgencies by separatist Kurds, Baluchis, and Turkomans. It was during the eight-year war with Iraq, however, that the IRGC matured and gradually developed its land, air, and sea divisions to become a full-fledged military force. The IRGC has the Basij, the most powerful paramilitary organization in Iran, under its wing. Today, it is believed to be the most powerful protector of Ayatollah Khomeini's revolutionary ideals and the strongest weapon in the hands of clergy.

MAJOR CRISES

Since its beginning, the Islamic Republic of Iran has faced many internal and external challenges. The most significant challenge came from the war with Iraq, a conflict that was both socially and economically disastrous for the nation. The second challenge came from the hostage crisis that antagonized the United States and impacted many of Iran's other foreign relations.

THE IRAN-IRAQ WAR

On September 22, 1980, Iraqi forces invaded Iran in an attempt to annex the Shatt-al-Arab (Arvand Rud) waterway that forms part of Iran's western border with Iraq. By Iraqi leader Saddam Hussein's calculation, Iran was too torn apart by revolution to defend itself against the Iraqi army. But that proved to be a serious miscalculation. Within a year, Iraqi forces were expelled from invaded territories and were on the defensive. The IRGC, along with the regular army and the volunteer militia (*basij*),

In 1980, shortly after the revolution that ousted Shah Mohammad Reza, the neighboring nation of Iraq invaded Iran, hoping for an easy victory. Iraqi leader Saddam Hussein's incorrectly assumed that Iran was too disorganized to defend herself, and a bloody conflict raged for eight years, ending in a standoff.

fought with revolutionary fervor and defeated the much better equipped Iraqi army. Iran, however, made a major mistake by continuing the war on Iraqi soil, hoping to overthrow Saddam's regime and replace it with a friendly one. The move was unsuccessful, however, and a bloody conflict dragged on for eight years, claiming an estimated one million lives and causing unbelievable hardship for millions of others on both sides.

THE HOSTAGE CRISIS

On November 4, 1979, militant Muslim students, demanding that the United States government return the exiled Shah—who had entered the country for medical treatment—to Iran, seized the American embassy in Tehran, taking 53 Americans hostage. The students said they would free the hostages when the Shah was handed over to Iran to face justice. Diplomatic relations between Iran and the United States were immediately severed. Washington did not return the Shah and retaliated by freezing over $10 million in Iranian assets held in the United States. The United States also attempted a military rescue that failed, resulting in the loss of eight American military personnel.

After 444 days of confinement, the United States struck a deal with the Iranian government and the hostages were released on the eve of President Ronald Reagan's inauguration. Many American political analysts believe that Jimmy Carter, who was running for reelection to the U.S. presidency, lost the election because of his handling of the hostage crisis.

U.S.–IRANIAN RELATIONS

Relations between the United States and Iran remain antagonistic. Each side uses the other as a political scapegoat to encourage the passage of expensive defense budgets and to rally support for political actions. In addition, commercial relations between the two countries are very limited, mainly due to U.S. economic sanctions against Iran.

The U.S. government's grievances against Iran range from Iran's support for international terrorism, its hostility toward Israel, and its acquisition of nuclear weapons and other weapons of mass destruction. Iran's grievances against the United States include America's support for Israeli occupation policies, its involvement in the affairs of Persian Gulf countries, the downing of an Iranian jetliner by American Navy missiles on July 3, 1988, killing 290 people, and the freezing of Iranian assets since the beginning of the Iranian revolution. By August 2002, there was no indication that relations between the two governments would improve soon, particularly following the terrorist attacks on the United States in September 2001. President George W. Bush, elected in 2000, included Iran on his list of "Axis of Evil" countries in his 2001 State of the Union address. Iran viewed this designation as evidence of an unwillingness to improve relations on the part of the United States.

RELATIONS WITH OTHER COUNTRIES

Iran generally has good relations with its neighbors, although it has had major conflicts in recent decades with Iraq and Afghanistan. Since the end of its long war with Iraq, relations between the two countries have improved. Currently, for example, Iranian pilgrims are now allowed to visit the holy Shiite cities in southern Iraq, and the two countries have exchanged prisoners of war. Also, since the end of the Taliban regime in Afghanistan, Iran has had a good relationship with that country. Relations with Gulf countries have improved significantly during Khatami's presidency. Although Iran and the United Arab Emirates have had disputes over some of the smaller Persian Gulf islands, their relations seem to be good.

Iran also has maintained friendly relations with Russia, who has been helping Iran with its economic development and supplying it with military equipment. Russia has also been involved in building a nuclear reactor in the southern Iranian city of Bushehr. The Chinese have helped Iran build major industrial plants and transportation facilities, and Iran's relations with Japan and some Western European countries also have been mutually beneficial.

Modernization has brought sharp contrasts to Iran's economy. Today, the country's traditional agricultural pursuits exist alongside the high-technology oil industry.

Economic Patterns

MODERNIZATION OF THE ECONOMY

Iran's traditional source of livelihood prior to the discovery of oil was agriculture, although some also earned income through trade, services, and craftsmanship. Primary exports included quality handicrafts, particularly textiles and carpets, as well as decorative gold, silver, copper, and brass items. But with the discovery of oil in 1908, petroleum gradually became the backbone of the country's economy.

With the emergence of the Pahlavi dynasty in 1925, the economy began to change again. Iran began to look toward European countries for models of development. Reza Shah attempted to modernize the country by stabilizing the central government, building an educational system, improving communications, and constructing roads and railways. The process of industrialization also began, though the emphasis was more on capital-intensive (machine-driven) rather than labor-intensive industries.

The process of modernization continued more aggressively under Mohammad Reza Shah after he replaced his father in 1941. By then the income from oil had increased and Iran had more educated professionals who could lead the nation to a more prosperous future. This Shah's regime significantly expanded the country's physical infrastructure by building more roads, railroads, ports, airports, and industries, and by improving communications and services for urban areas. Until 1978, the economy was doing very well. The annual growth rate between 1960 and 1977 was around 10 percent—outstanding for a developing country.

Financial prosperity, however, was not reaching the needy people and only a small percentage of the population benefited. Also, the Shah's immense appetite for militarization diverted the country's modernization focus, and a huge amount of money was spent to buy different types of armaments, particularly from the United States. The Shah's government failed to improve human conditions. He did not make the political system more democratic, nor improve the economic system by reducing the strong grip of economic monopolies. Neither did he reduce governmental corruption, or develop programs to help the poor and dispossessed. His failure in these areas was a primary factor contributing to the 1979 mass uprising which brought the Islamic Republic to power.

Islamization of Economy

The 1979 revolution that brought the clerics to power seriously disrupted Iran's development and economic growth. The revolutionary government had no real economic plan. It simply wanted to reverse many of the former regime's ongoing policies. The government began to take over major industries from their private managers. And it confiscated many enterprises which were owned by the Shah's sympathizers. The revolutionaries' main goal was to change the nature of the development plans from what they called "Westernized" to what they considered to be "Islamized." They "Islamized" Iranian banks by making them nonprofit organizations and giving interest-free loans (making money by collecting interest is forbidden in Islamic law).

In the name of confronting Westernization, the government stopped the import of luxury goods from Western countries and cut funding for many existing development and construction projects. Iran, according to revolutionaries, needed to become self-reliant and independent from superpower intervention.

Ideology versus Efficiency

Soon a group of revolutionary conglomerates known as *bonyads* (foundations) were given a free hand by the government. They rapidly monopolized Iran's main economic enterprises. According to these bonyads, individuals with a revolutionary Islamic ideology were better suited to manage the country's main institutions than were secular professionals. So it was "ideology," rather than "efficiency" and know-how, which became the main qualifier for employment. In the name of ideology, a large number of well-educated professionals were fired from universities, courts, and other institutions and were replaced by ideologues known as "insiders" by revolutionaries. This approach led to a serious "brain drain" through the emigration of a huge number of skilled professionals, managers, and entrepreneurs from the country. Today, more than three million Iranians live abroad, many of whom left following the revolution.

Impeding External Factors

There also were external forces that had a negative impact on the Iranian economy during the first decade following the revolution. These factors included the Iran-Iraq war, a drop in the price of oil, Western economic sanctions against the country, and the freezing of billions of dollars of Iranian assets abroad.

War with Iraq was the most damaging factor; nearly all of Iran's oil income went directly to cover war expenses. The preoccupation with war also set back the process of industrialization and economic development.

ECONOMY DURING THE 1990s

By the late 1980s, when Iran had already reached a cease-fire agreement with Iraq and the revolutionary fever had cooled down somewhat, the government began to realize its past mistakes and looked for a new approach to economic development. By the early 1990s, the government started to privatize some small industries and invite both Iranians living abroad and non-Iranian investors to conduct business in Iran. But there were also many problems that discouraged such investment. Iranian business laws were easily subject to abuse and manipulation. Corruption was widespread within government and the bonyads. Government conservatism discouraged many potential investors, as did the country's gross mismanagement of matters pertaining to both politics and economics.

Khatami's Reforms

Most observers now believe that the economy stagnated because of the country's revolutionary political structure that placed power in the hands of those who directly benefited from chaotic economic and political conditions. The 1997 election of Mohammad Khatami as Iranian president was interpreted by some as a possible chance to liberalize the country's political and economic establishments. Khatami called for a total restructuring of the Iranian economy during the country's latest five-year plan (between 2000 and 2005). He announced a grand program to privatize several major industries such as communications, postal service, railways, and petrochemicals. The five-year plan also sought to create 750,000 new jobs each year and to achieve an average annual increase in the gross domestic product (GDP) of 6 percent.

The plan attempts to reduce subsidies for basic commodities

(including bread, rice, sugar, vegetable oil, wheat, and fuels), and introduce a range of fiscal and structural reforms. Although the progress so far has not been significant, the GNP did grow by 4.3 percent in 2001, and it was expected to be around 3.5 percent in 2002.

Necessity for Foreign Investment

Many Iranian economists believe that opening the country to foreign investment will boost the economy and contribute to a much-needed advance in the acceptance and use of different kinds of modern technology. To assure the security of investments made in Iran by foreign companies, parliament passed a law exempting those overseas companies operating in an offshore free-trade zone from threats of nationalization. But in November 1999 the law was rejected by the conservative Guardian Council. In May 2001, a "Law of Attraction and Protection of Foreign Investment" was passed by the parliament. But it, too, was rejected by the Guardian Council. As of August 2002, major disagreements still existed between the parliament and the Guardian Council concerning acceptance of foreign investment in Iran. While there are some foreign investors in the country, the issue is how (or whether) to encourage more such investment to "jump start" the stagnant economy.

Population Growth, Poverty, and Unemployment

Rapid population growth, particularly during the 1980s, directly hindered economic growth and development in Iran. At the time of the 1979 revolution, 36 million people lived in the country. By 2002, this number had increased to approximately 70 million, 65 percent of whom were under 25 years of age. This young and demanding population has placed tremendous pressure on Iran's economy, services, and resources. Job prospects are limited and unemployment is high. The officially announced unemployment rate in early 2002 was 14 percent, but according to private sources it was much higher.

According to a 2002 report by the Central Bank of Iran, the cost of living for families in urban areas amounted to 2.3 million Rials, or $287.50 ($1 = 8000 Rials), per month while the monthly average income of government employees was only 1 million Rials, or $125. This means that if both husband and wife work, they will still be living under the poverty level. In 2002, over 50 percent of Iranians lived under the poverty level. Many people, particularly those living in large cities with high rents, must hold multiple jobs just to get by.

Wealth Distribution

Many Iranians complain that a major goal of the 1979 revolution—to achieve a more equitable distribution of wealth—has not been achieved. A 2002 report by Iran's Plan and Budget Organization disclosed that the wealthiest 20 percent of the population holds 50 percent of the gross national product (GNP) and the 40 percent at the bottom of the income pyramid holds only 16 percent of GNP. The lack of progress in addressing problems of poverty, unemployment, and inflation, not to mention harassment by the so-called moral police (conservative clergy), have led to frequent street riots by Iranian youth during 2001 and 2002. Administration of social and economic justice, many Iranians believe, should be the primary goal of the country's Economic Reconstruction Plan.

Government's Accomplishments

On the positive side, the government has succeeded in reducing the country's previously soaring birthrate and improving health conditions. Mortality rates are now significantly lower than during prerevolutionary times. For example, the infant mortality rate (number of children per 1,000 dying before reaching one year of age) has fallen from 104 in the 1970s to 25 in 2002. Life expectancy has increased from 55 to 70 years during the same period. Today, access to health facilities is easily available to most Iranians and government has kept the

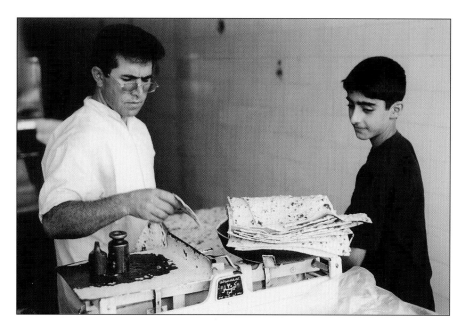

Iran's growing population has placed great pressure on the natural resources of the country. Despite oil-rich lands, more than half of Iran's citizens live below the poverty level. Here, a boy buys bread at a local market.

cost of medicine and medical treatments low. There are also many colleges and universities, and the literacy rate has grown significantly for both men and women. Today, some 72 percent of the people over age 15 can read and write.

Oil-Dependent Economy

Iran's economy is highly dependent on the country's vast oil reserves and production. Oil production is government controlled. Without oil revenues, Iran's economy would collapse. This dependency has made the economy very fragile, since changes in the price of oil can directly impact the country's five-year development plans. For example, in 1998, when the oil price fell below $10 a barrel, the country's economy was on the verge of collapse. Fortunately, the oil price rebounded and the economy was able to stabilize, including its ability to pay foreign debts. When a country relies on a single commodity as its primary source of livelihood, it is very much at the mercy of the buyers. If buyers boycott the commodity, then the economy will collapse under pressure. The 1953 international boycott of Iranian oil weakened the Musaddeq government, allowing it to be easily overthrown by a low-budget CIA-orchestrated coup. Today, Iranian economists seek economic diversification, which they believe is essential for the country's future well-being.

RESOURCES AND INDUSTRIES

Oil

Iran sits upon two of the world's most productive oil fields, those of the Caspian Depression to the north and the Persian Gulf to the south. The country's oil reserves are estimated to be 90 billion barrels, or roughly 9 percent of world's total. Most of Iran's crude oil reserves are located in giant onshore fields along a northwest–southeast belt running parallel to the Zagros Mountains. Khuzestan province is particularly known for its oil production. Among the most active fields are Ahwaz-Bangestan, Marun, Gachsaran, Agha Jari, and Bibi Hakimeh. During 2001, Iran produced about 3.9 million barrels per day, of which 1.1 million barrels were used for domestic consumption and 2.8 million were exported. About 600,000 barrels per day of the total production came from offshore fields. The government is currently working on improving and expanding offshore production.

Natural Gas

Iran ranks second behind Russia in proven reserves of natural gas. Deposits are estimated at 812 trillion cubic feet, about 15 percent of the world total. Most gas fields are located in the same areas as the oil deposits. Unlike the oil fields, however, most of the gas fields have not yet been developed. Iran hopes to increase production and become a major exporter of natural gas. In 2000, most of the 2.1 million cubic feet of natural gas produced was used for domestic consumption.

Around half of Iran's current total energy consumption comes from natural gas. Domestic consumption of this clean-burning fuel is expected to increase by 70 percent by the year 2005.

Non-Oil Resources

Other Iranian resources include the metals iron, copper, zinc, lead, chromite, and manganese. There also are abundant reserves of such building materials as limestone, marble, clay, and construction rock. Other materials of use include glass sand, salt, kaolin, turquoise, coal, and sulfur. A recent use of satellite imagery helped in the discovery of a highly mineralized volcanic belt near the tectonic plate boundary along the inner Zagros range, roughly paralleling the railroad linking the cities of Qom and Kerman. This belt includes iron, chrome, lead, zinc, bauxite, manganese, coal, barite, and a massive amount of copper. Copper, with deposits estimated to be 2.6 billion tons, is Iran's most important non-oil resource in terms of international trade.

Industries

Prerevolutionary industries ranged from food processing to iron and steel production and automobile assembly. During the Shah's regime, joint ventures with foreign corporations resulted in the transfer of some Western technology and in training programs for Iranian labors and managers. Following the 1979 revolution, industrial production suffered greatly. Among the disruptions were political conditions themselves, a shortage of spare parts, an unreliable labor force, emigration of many capable industrial managers, and the war with Iraq. When the war with Iraq ended, industrial production gradually began to rebound.

Petroleum and refining remains the country's main industry. Iran is a key member of the Organization of Petroleum Exporting Countries (OPEC). It has about nine oil refineries with a total capacity of 1.2 million barrels per day. The largest is in Abadan, near the border with Iraq. During the 1980 Iraqi invasion, this refinery was nearly destroyed and its 400,000-barrel-per-day production ceased. By the late 1980s, however, the refinery resumed full production. Other major refineries are located in Esfahan, Bander-e Abbas, and Tehran.

Iran also has many important non-oil-related industries. They include the manufacture of textiles, food processing, and sugar refining; iron and steel milling and automobile assembly; petrochemical, fertilizer, cement, building material, and machine tool production. The country also produces a variety of household items and appliances, beverages, cigarettes, inlaid items, decorated ceramic tiles, and Persian rugs and carpets.

The Tehran metropolitan area, including Karaj, is the country's largest industrial core. It is home to most of the automobile assembly plants, household appliance factories, and clothing factories. Esfahan, in central Iran, is the second-largest industrial center, containing the country's major iron and steel plants. Esfahan is also particularly famous for its artisans, who create its hand-knotted carpets and artistically decorated metal household items such as brass and copper trays. Tabriz is the industrial center of northwest Iran, producing tractors and other major machine tools. Iran's largest aluminum smelter is located in Arak. Many Iranian cities in addition to Esfahan are known for their carpet production; among the most important ones are Tabriz, Kerman, Nain, Qom, Kashan, Mashhad, and Hamadan.

AGRICULTURE

Although only 10 percent of Iranian land is arable (suited to farming), agriculture still employs about a quarter of the labor force and accounts for one-fifth of the GDP. In a dry region such as Middle East, Iran has managed to become a viable agricultural country, producing crops and livestock. In fact, agriculture was the fastest-growing sector of the Iranian economy during much of 1990s. Crops are produced both through dry farming (rain-fed) and irrigation schemes. Forms of irrigation include diverting river water through a network of

The weaving of fine handmade carpets is a traditional pursuit in many areas. Craftsmen in the city of Esfahan produce carpets as well as brass and copper household items.

canals, digging deep wells, and the *qanat* system (see Chapter 2). Qanats have been a significant source of water for crop production in the arid regions of Iran.

Today Iran is the Middle East's leading producer of oranges, dates, melons, sheep, goats, and chickens. Wheat, barley, and rice are the dominant Iranian crops. While wheat and barley are produced almost all over the country in both rain-fed and irrigated areas, rice production is limited to moist areas bordering the Caspian Sea. Other crops include cotton, sugar beets, tea, cumin, hemp, tobacco, and saffron. Due to its large and growing population, Iran must import a significant amount of food, particularly wheat and rice.

Iran's abundant fruit and nut crops provide valuable food sources and are exported throughout the world. After oil and carpets, these crops are the third-largest Iranian export. In an Iranian fruit market like this one, you can find grapes, peaches, plums, figs, melons, and a range of other delicious items.

Tree crops are also common in Iran. The country is the world's largest producer of pistachio nuts. Varieties of pistachios are produced in different regions of Iran. Among other nuts produced are almonds, walnuts, and hazelnuts. Nuts and dried fruits are the third most important Iranian export in terms of value after oil and carpets. Due to abundant sunshine, Iranian fruits are very tasty. Iranians who live in other countries cannot wait to visit their homeland in summertime to taste the variety of delicious grapes, peaches, plums, oranges, figs, sweet and sour cherries, mulberries, and several varieties of sweet melons.

LIVESTOCK, FISHING, AND FORESTRY

The Mediterranean climate allows for good pastures in Iran for raising livestock. Pastures cover 27 percent of Iran's total land area. Sheep, goats, and cattle grazing in green pastures are a common sight that a traveler through Iran is sure to notice. Besides meat, animals are used for their milk, wool, hair, and hides. In the case of cattle, the manure is used as fertilizer and dried for use as fuel in rural villages.

Fishing is mainly done in the Caspian Sea, along the Persian Gulf coast, and in the Gulf of Oman. Fish caught in the Persian Gulf and the Gulf of Oman includes sardines, sole, tuna, snapper, and swordfish. Shrimp also are taken from these waters. The Caspian Sea is known for its supply of whitefish, white salmon, carp, bream, pike, catfish, and sturgeon. Sturgeon is a valuable fish, since it is the source of the roe that is processed into caviar. Iran is one of the world's largest suppliers of caviar, and Iranian caviar is recognized as being the finest in the world. Caviar, along with the spice saffron, are luxury items that visitors to Iran often take back with them to their families and friends.

Forestry has been an important land use particularly along the northern slopes of the Elburz Mountains. Due to abundant rainfall and mild climate there, dense forests cover these slopes. Caspian forests include hardwoods such as oak, beech, maple, elm, ash, walnut, fig, and alder, and a variety of scrub. There are also forests covering the western slopes of the Zagros Mountains and the slopes of Khorasan province. With the exception of Turkey, Iran has the only commercially productive forests in the Middle East.

TRANSPORTATION

Iran serves as a bridge connecting Europe, Central Asia, and the Caucasus with the Persian Gulf and Indian Ocean to the south. Although Iran's mountainous nature makes construction of national roads and railroads difficult and costly, the country does have a relatively well-established transportation network. A systematic highway network connects most major cities. It also connects to the roads in neighboring countries to the north, east, and west. There are about 110,000 miles (177,000 kilometers) of roads, of which 1,360 miles (2,189 kilometers) are highways with at least four lanes.

With its long coastlines along the Persian Gulf, Gulf of Oman, and Caspian Sea, Iran contains many ports, called *bandar* in Persian. The major southern ports include Shaheed Rajayee, with an annual capacity of 13 million tons, and Shaheed Beheshti and Bushehr, each with a capacity of 2 million tons. Among major ports along the Caspian Sea are Anzali and Nowshahr, both with a capacity of 1.0 to 1.5 million tons. According to Iranian government figures, the country's annual port capacity is around 42 million tons. Over 4,300 miles (6,920 kilometers) of railroad track connect these ports to other Iranian cities. Iran's shipping lines and the National Oil Tanker Company are among the world's leading marine carriers.

Iran is also well connected to the rest of the world through airways. There are over 300 airports, about 120 of which have paved runways. Mehrabad Airport near Tehran is the nation's largest in terms of carriers, flights, and passengers.

TRADE AND TRADE PARTNERS

As already mentioned, petroleum is Iran's major export. It accounted for some 85 percent of the country's $25 billion export trade during 2000. Customers vary from year to year, although the most reliable are Japan, the United Kingdom, Germany, South Korea, and Turkey. Other significant exports include carpets, fruits and nuts (pistachio, raisins, and dates), animal hides, caviar, petrochemicals, textiles, garments, and other food products.

Major imports include industrial machinery, iron and steel products, transport equipment, foodstuffs (mainly grains), textiles, pharmaceuticals, chemical products, and military supplies. The total value of imports for the year 2000 was around $15 billion. Major import partners are Japan, Italy, Germany, United Arab Emirates, South Korea, France, China, and Russia. Due to U.S. economic sanctions against Iranian goods, there is no major trade between the two nations.

ENVIRONMENTAL PROBLEMS

Iranian cities, particularly large metropolitan areas such as Tehran, Esfahan, and Tabriz, suffer from a variety of environmental problems caused by transportation and industrial pollution. Air pollution, especially in Tehran, is the most serious man-made environmental problem. Primary sources included vehicle emissions, refinery operations, and industrial plants. The level of lead concentration in Tehran's air is so high that occasionally the government asks citizens to stay inside or wear masks for safety. Pollution related to oil production in the Persian Gulf areas also is a significant problem. Soil erosion and depletion are widespread, due to overgrazing and inefficient agricultural practices. Deforestation also has become a problem due to illegal cutting and inadequate forest management. Other problems relating to the natural environment include earthquakes, droughts, floods, sand and dust storms, and water shortages.

The family unit is extremely important in Iranian society. This Iranian family watches a soccer match on television. Soccer is a popular sport in the country and watching the matches is a favorite entertainment for people of all ages.

Life in
Iran Today

I ranian society is becoming more and more divided in several ways. It is a society characterized by religious groups versus secular factions; urban dwellers versus rural population; traditional beliefs versus a westernized outlook; and finally, the rich versus poor. All of these groups, however, do have one thing in common: the importance of family. In the West, the individual tends to be the focus of society. In Iran, as elsewhere in the Middle East, society and societal laws focus much more on the family.

THE FAMILY

Family forms the basic unit of Iranian society. The unit is defined by a series of principles that are recognized by most Iranians even when they live abroad. The father is usually the head of the household. He is responsible for the family's well-being. This goes beyond merely financial support; he is responsible for family members' social and spiritual needs as well. He is the authority and disciplinarian of the house, so he demands obedience. Since other family members look up to him, the father must be a good role model. If he goes "astray" in some way, the entire family will suffer the consequences.

Of course, this latter tradition is also true for the mother. The mother is especially considered a role model for daughters. She is very much the moral gauge of the family. She is supposed to raise good children and instill good values in them. The Prophet Mohammad said, "Heaven is at the feet of mothers." This saying and many similar proverbs and comments found in Iranian secular and religious literature have greatly elevated the status of mothers in Iranian society. Usually when a woman reaches the status of a mother she is much more respected by others.

The great importance placed on motherhood has put a lot of pressure on childless women. Recently, a popular Iranian movie, *Leila*, focused on this dilemma. In the film, Leila is a charming and educated but childless woman who is pressured by her husband's family to choose a second wife for her husband. Officially, Islam allows men to marry up to four wives, and the new Islamic government has made it easier for Iranian men to do so. This has created hot debates among Iranian intellectuals. The Qu'ran emphasizes that a man who decides to marry more than one wife should be able to treat them equally. But it also notes that this is often impossible. Some critics of the practice believe that a systematic interpretation of Islamic verses discourages polygamy. However, although allowed, polygamy is rarely practiced today in Iran. Traditionally there has been a stigma attached to the practice, and educated men rarely choose multiple wives. Today, some women even put a clause relating to polygamy in their marriage agreement, indicating that the husband cannot have another wife.

MARRIAGE

How do Iranian youth find their mates? It really depends on the social, economic, and religious status of their families. Among traditional families, especially in smaller towns and rural areas, it is customary that the family of the groom finds a prospective bride. Of course, there are various criteria for selecting a suitable mate. Usually the mate is chosen from a similar socioeconomic class and religious background. The family's reputation in the neighborhood is the most important factor in bride selection and, for that matter, in the groom's desirability as well. Chances of finding a husband from a decent family are significantly reduced, for example, if the proposed bride's mother does not have a good reputation.

If the reputation of the bride's family somehow matches that of the groom's family, then the parents of the groom (mainly the female members such as mother, sister, and aunts) visit the bride's house. Here the family of the bride has to be on its best behavior so that the groom's family will leave their house with a good impression. Among the things that the groom's family are concerned with are the cleanliness of the house, good taste in decoration, the quality of service given to guests, and, of greatest importance, the family's mannerisms and level of politeness.

Of course, during this meeting the family of the bride also scrutinizes the family of their potential son-in-law. Toward the end of the meeting, through their conversation and mannerisms, the parties indicate whether they are willing to hold a future meeting. If there is a mutual liking between the two families, the groom's family requests another meeting. The next meeting could be outside the house with chaperones or another visit to bride's house. The couple is given an opportunity to converse and find out about each other. If things go well, the next step is the engagement, usually a small ceremony held in the presence of the couple's close family and friends. If things still progress positively, marriage usually takes place a year or two later. The size of the wedding celebration depends on the socioeconomic status of the families involved.

Arranged marriages occur less frequently among middle- and upper-class educated families. As is the case in the West, couples often meet at parties, or at public places such as colleges, parks, or movie theatres. When there is a clear mutual attraction and interest, then the parents become involved in conducting formalities.

Marriages are conducted by the Shiite clerics, or by licensed individuals. Unlike Christian marriage ceremonies, which usually are conducted in a church, Iranian Muslim marriages are not done in mosques (Muslim churches). Of course, Muslims are encouraged to marry Muslims. They cannot marry people who practice polytheistic religions. A Muslim woman can only marry a Muslim man (although he may be a convert to the faith). However, Muslim men can marry women of other monotheistic religions such as Christianity, Judaism, or Zoroastrianism. In multireligious marriages, the marriage has to be conducted in Islamic fashion and the non-Muslim spouse takes a Muslim name.

Marriage is a contract between the two families. There is always *mahreyyeh* (money or property deed), which can be loosely translated as the bride's price. After some preliminary negotiations, elders of the two families agree on the amount of mahreyyeh. It can be in cash, gold coins, or deed to certain properties. The size of mahreyyeh again depends on the socioeconomic status of the families involved. The rationale behind mahreyyeh is to secure the bride's status in the groom's house. In the case of divorce initiated by a husband, he must transfer mahreyyeh to the wife.

Mahreyyeh legally belongs to the wife and she can cash it anytime during the marriage at her request. Traditionally, however, it is transferred to the wife only in cases of divorce or the husband's death or disappearance. Some women choose to use

The role of women in Iran has grown in recent decades, compared with other Arab neighbors. Many women receive advanced education, both inside and outside the country, and many are employed in skilled jobs outside the home. Here we see women musicians in Iran's national orchestra.

it for the education of their children. In the Iranian legal system, women and men can both initiate divorce, but usually this step is much easier for the husband to initiate than the wife.

STATUS OF WOMEN

Compared with their counterparts in Arab countries, Iranian women have achieved significant rights. They are generally well-educated and have occupied many professional positions traditionally filled by men. Many government clerics do not believe in the equality of men and women, but the assertiveness of Iranian women, supported by some enlightened clerics like President Khatami, has paved the way for women's further professional achievement. In a recent speech,

Khatami indicated that according to Islam there is no differ-ence between men and women. To prove his statement he selected Masoumeh Ebtekar, an Iranian woman educated in the United States, as one of his vice-presidents.

Women were very influential in the election of Khatami, both in 1997 and 2001. They campaigned and voted for Khatami and other reformist parliamentary candidates. Recently, another popular Ayatollah also publicly declared that there should be nothing to stop women from becoming president or even the supreme religious leader. This statement was very significant, because the position of Supreme Leader is believed to be ordained by God.

Despite all the progress, under Iranian law women still are not exactly equal to men. There are a number of discrim-inatory laws that women activists and their supporters would like to change. For example, a woman's testimony in court is worth only half that of a man's, and in terms of blood money (paid when a person is murdered or killed by accident), the value of woman's life is half of a man's. Women also are not allowed to be judges, but they can be attorneys at the court. But the most discriminatory law relates to child custody and distribution of wealth in cases of divorce or death of a husband. Often, men get custody unless children are very young. And in the case of a husband's death, the husband's father, rather than his wife, can get the custody of children and authority over his son's assets.

Many Iranian women also complain about the strict dress codes that have been imposed on them by the government since the 1979 revolution. Before the revolution, women could appear in public in Western dress. Whether or not to wear the traditional Islamic head veil was a personal choice. Under the new government, women are only allowed to display their face, hands, and toes in public. In larger cities, most women wear scarves and lose garments to cover their body curves. However, the government's moral police's preference is the *chador,* a tentlike veil covering the body from head to toe. However, women do not always observe dress rules and they are frequently stopped and warned by the cruising moral police in public places.

ART AND LITERATURE

Although in the West Iran is known for its political upheavals and revolutionary fervor, most Iranians see politics as an ever-changing wave. They simply try to adjust as well as they can. Meanwhile, like everybody else, they live their daily lives and try to fulfill their spiritual needs as well as their material necessities. Perhaps the most obvious aesthetic face of Iranian culture is its art and poetry. Iranians have a deep appreciation of art. Seeing a beautiful Persian carpet with delicate coloring and design, a ceramic bowl with exquisite patterns, a charming miniature painting decorated by delightful calligraphy, or an attractive garden will stimulate their artistic senses and add to the quality of their lives.

The American scholar Arthur Pope, in his six-volume classic, *A Survey of Persian Art,* eloquently explains Persian art and architecture. Pope spent a good portion of his life in Iran and was taken by the architectural beauty of the numerous mosques and palaces that he visited. A beautiful blue dome against a brownish mountain in the background is an image that an artistic mind won't easily forget. Many Iranians who live abroad crave returning home to once again see the beautiful places of their past memories. They long to see the majestic Persepolis in the sunset, the mosques and palaces of Esfahan, and the shrine of Imam Reza in Mashhad. They dream of cruising on the mysterious and puzzling waters of the Alisadr caverns around Hamadan, spending a summer evening on the slopes of Darband in northern Tehran, and contemplating the tombs of Hafez and Sadi, their favorite Iranian poets, while quietly whispering their poems.

Iranian works of art are not always kept in museums. They are also displayed in public for the enjoyment of passersby. City squares may have posters that include poems written in exquisite Persian calligraphy and accompanied by beautiful paintings or drawings. The content of most of the displayed poetry is about love and spiritual maturity. Far from being political, these posters display the poetic heart of the nation.

POETRY

To those who are familiar with the world's poetic and romantic literature, Iran is known as the "land of flowers and nightingales." Numerous Iranian poets have written sizzling tales of love affairs between legendary lovers. This love is often compared symbolically to the unconditional love of the nightingale for the flower, or the sacrificial passion of the moth for the flame. Long before Shakespeare wrote his masterpiece *Romeo and Juliet*, the famous Iranian poet Nezami (died 1202 A.D.) wrote his sensational tale of Leili and Majnon, the two lovers from conflicting social, economic, and political backgrounds who struggled to save their love against all odds. It is possible that the romantic tale of Leili and Majnon was Shakespeare's inspiration for writing his celebrated *Romeo and Juliet*.

There are many other romantic tales from various periods of Iranian literary history that are among the most commonly read literature by the Iranian population. Today, many Iranians seek refuge in the warmth of the uplifting and mediating poetry of Hafez (died 1389 A.D.), the legendary Iranian poet whose work is used in the art of fortune-telling.

The Iranian poets most widely read in the United States are Rumi (died 1273 A.D.), known for his insightful Sufi poetry, and Omar Khayyam (died 1131 A.D.) for his enriching philosophical poetry. In reality, Rumi has remained the most-read foreign poet in the United States for over a decade. His work can be found in the form of books and audiotapes in any major bookstore. The impact of poetry on Iranian culture is so staggering that one can listen to an everyday conversation among Iranians and hear lines of poetry used in their expressions and arguments.

Iran is also a land of great scientists and philosophers. Among them were Khwarazmi, Razi, and Avicenna. Khwarazmi, a ninth-century mathematician and astronomer, wrote the first work of algebra. The word "algebra" is derived from his books; the word "algorithm" comes from a distortion of his name. Zakareyya Razi, a great scientist and physician living between the ninth and tenth centuries, is known for his discovery of alcohol and his books on curing smallpox and measles. Ibn Sina (Avicenna) lived between the tenth and eleventh centuries and wrote over 200 books, including *The Canon of Medicine*, an encyclopedia summarizing all the known medical knowledge at the time from across the world. This work, through its translated versions, remained the most influential book of medicine in the world until the seventeenth century.

The Iranian cultural landscape today is dotted with the tombs and shrines of famous poets, writers, scientists, and philosophers. They far outnumber the shrines of politicians and military figures.

CINEMA

Iranian artists and intellectuals have also shown their creativity in areas of the modern arts. Today, Iranian cinema is considered to be among the world's most progressive.

Prerevolutionary cinema was very popular in Iran, and some Iranian movies managed to win international awards, even though Iranian cinema was not yet globally known. The postrevolutionary Iranian cinema, however, has captured the world's attention. Every year several Iranian movies win awards from the most respectable film festivals and they are played in theatres around the world. In major American cities, Iranian films are shown frequently, and in some cases there are film festivals focusing on the work of successful Iranian directors.

Cinema has become a medium in which Iranian intellectuals can express their fears and aspirations and share their stories with their countrymen and the rest of the world. It has become a way of diffusing Iranian culture to other parts of the world. Many Americans who saw Majid Majidi's tender movie *Children of Heaven* talked for weeks about the impoverished little Ali and Zahra, the brother and sister who had to share the same pair of sneakers. This cinematic tale was one of the five candidates for the 1999 Academy Award for Best Foreign Film. In 1997, Kiarostami's *Taste of Cherry*, the story of despair over Iran's social structure, won the first-place Palm d'Or award at the international Cannes film festival. In 2000, three Iranian movies won prizes at Cannes; one of them was *Apple*, a movie by Samira Makhmalbaf, a 20-year-old Iranian woman. She was the youngest award winner in the festival's history.

Today there are over twenty directors whose movies have captured the attention of their colleagues throughout the world. Among them are Tahmine Milani and Rakhshan Banni-Etemad, both of whom have been particularly successful in demonstrating the problems of Iranian women and society at large under the Islamic Republic's government. Milani has been imprisoned by the regime for her aggressive criticism of government policies. Her movies, especially *Two Women* and *The Hidden Half*, have been praised by many throughout the world. It is interesting that the Islamic government at first promoted the motion picture industry for propaganda purposes. Today, however, the industry has become one of the most outspoken critics of government policies. While intellectual movies are not always successful at the local box office, young people from high schools, colleges, and universities are among the regular viewers.

SPORTS

Sport has always been popular in Iran. There are tales of Iranian youth competing with Greeks during ancient Olympics. Among traditional sports practiced in Iran are horseback riding, wrestling, fencing, archery, and polo. Today the most popular sports are soccer (called football in Iran), weight lifting, and different styles of wrestling. Iranian wrestlers are among the best in the world, and they have won many medals in international competitions. The Iranian national soccer team is one of the best in Asia, and many Iranian athletes play for European professional teams.

EDUCATION

Another success story of postrevolutionary Iran has been its educational system. Educating the public has been a government priority. Today, an estimated 70 to 80 percent of Iranians can read and almost all children go to school. Public schools are free. In Iran, however, private schools often provide students with a better quality education. There are national-standard tests that primary, middle, and high school students must pass in order to move to the next step.

Admission to college or university can be difficult. Although the number of institutions of higher education has increased since the revolution, so has the college-age population. There simply is not enough space for all young people seeking to further their education. Applicants must take a difficult entrance exam, called the "conquer." High school students devote much of their last two years preparing for this exam. Newspapers publish the test results in midsummer. Those long, hot days before the announcement of results are known as "days of destiny" for many Iranian youth. Those who fail the test usually try the next calendar year. If they fail again, they must do their two-year compulsory military service, which is required for Iranian males when they reach 21 years of age.

Iran's post-revolutionary educational system has achieved great successes. Iran's public schools have boosted the country's literacy rate to about eighty percent. Students must successfully pass nationally standardized tests in the primary, middle, and high schools in order to move ahead to the next step in their education.

IRANIAN CALENDAR

The Iranian calendar is based on solar activity. The year begins at the spring equinox, when the length of day and night are equal throughout the world. Since it takes the Earth 365 days, 5 hours, 49 minutes, and 4 seconds to complete one revolution around the sun, the Iranian New Year does not fall on the same day every year; it moves between March 19 and March 22.

The Iranian calendar also displays the Islamic nature of Iran. It is called *Hejri-e Shamsi*, meaning the solar calendar based on migration. Year one of this calendar is 622 A.D., the year that the Prophet Mohammad migrated from Mecca to Medina in the Arabian peninsula, where he established the first Islamic community. The official Iranian week starts on Saturday and ends on Friday. According to Muslims, God created Earth in six days and rested on Friday, so Friday became the Muslim holiday. Iranians usually take Thursday afternoon off, to make a longer weekend. On Thursday evening many Iranian Muslims visit cemeteries and pray for their deceased relatives and friends.

NO-ROOZ

No-Rooz is the greatest Persian festival for Iranians throughout the world. The name comes from *no*, meaning "new," and *rooz*, meaning "day," or New Day. It is a joyous celebration of nature's rejuvenation. The long, cold winter has passed and spring, the season of rebirth, has arrived. Iranians have celebrated this 13-day festival for some 3,000 years. On the thirteenth day, families go picnicking in open fields. Young men and women tie the grass, hoping that by the time the knot is open they will meet their future mates. Although Persian in origin, No-Rooz is celebrated by nearly all Iranian cultures.

Iran is a young nation—over half her population is under 20 years of age. Faced with this recent population explosion, poverty, and the currently precarious political relationship with Western nations, its people look to a future filled with challenges.

9

Iran
Looks Ahead

Buzzing Tehran, Iran's populous capital with its seven million people, is one of the busiest cities of the world. It is a city of contrasts. Wide boulevards, highways, and metros in the newly expanded city stand in sharp contrast to the narrow winding streets of the old quarters. The city leaves a variety of visual impressions in the minds of visitors. New skyscrapers imitating the architectural designs of the West stand in sharp contrast to old courtyard houses characterizing traditional folk architecture of the Middle East. Snow-capped peaks limit the northern expansion of the city, but provide Tehran with a splendid year-round view. In winter, ski resorts along the hillsides are popular attractions for skiers and people who simply want to get out of the crowded city and breathe fresh mountain air.

Billboards and pictures posted on walls facing streets and

highways tell of the country's recent turbulent history. Revolutionary propaganda, sponsored mainly by the government, still can be seen all over the city. There are pictures of revolutionary clerics who have held political positions at various times during the postrevolutionary period. There are photos of many martyrs of the bloody Iran-Iraq war, which took the lives of several hundred thousand young Iranian and Iraqi men. And, of course, there are anti-American slogans and propaganda that attest to the Islamic Republic's defiance of perceived American imperialistic intentions. All of these are visual reminders of the political changes that have occurred in Iran since the 1979 revolution.

The famous slogan of the revolution, "Neither East, nor West," is still seen on the walls. The East, meaning today's Russia, has been neutralized over time. It appears no longer intent on spreading communism and conquering neighboring lands. The Iranian government, however, is still suspicious of the United States—the West. During the American military operations in Afghanistan in 2001 and 2002, Iranian officials were nervous; now they are worried about American plans for Iraq. They see Iran as the next possible American target since the country has been included among President George W. Bush's "Axis of Evil" nations.

Although many Iranians dislike the current regime in Iran, they despise the idea of another foreign intervention. They have not forgotten that their dreams of freedom and democratic government were crushed by the CIA-supported coup of 1953: when they finally managed to release themselves from the ruling monarchy, with the opportunity to establish a prodemocratic government under the popular leadership of Musaddeq, the CIA intervened. As a result, Iranians realized that foreign countries look out for their own national interests. Thus, if political change is needed, they believe, it should come from within the country itself, and within the guidelines of its ruling system. America's unconditional support of the Shah at the expense of Iranian people's freedom created a negative image of the United States government in the minds of Iranian intellectuals. Dissatisfaction with the Shah's government inevitably led to a nationwide uprising which eventually forced the Shah out of Iran and paved the way for the current Islamic Republic.

Today, more than two decades after the revolution, the country faces a variety of social, political, and economic problems. Though there have been improvements in the lives of rural people and public education, the government's overwhelming corruption and disrespect for democracy have disappointed many of the old revolutionary sympathizers. Many people do not like the government's strict implementation of Islamic dress codes for women and sexual segregation of youth in public. There is also widespread concern about the increasing political oppression of intellectuals. The shortage of job opportunities has created an atmosphere of uncertainty and mistrust that far overshadows lingering anti-American feelings.

Iranians face an uncertain future. The problems enumerated above are causing many Iranian youth to consider leaving the country—particularly for the United States. It is evident that the political billboards do not necessarily exemplify the fears and aspirations of all Tehran residents.

Some recent Iranian motion picture themes express the frustration of Iranian youth in the face of unnecessary harassment by the government's moral police. A 2001-released Iranian movie, *The Swan's Song (Awaz e Qo)*, presents a tragic tale of a young Iranian couple forced to leave the country just to escape the government's harassment. Many thoughtful Iranians are puzzled about the government's unnecessary preoccupation with the behavior of youth while the country is suffering from serious economic and social problems. The Iranian currency has depreciated more than 100 times since prerevolutionary times. A U.S. dollar was worth 7 Iranian *tomans* in 1979; now, it is worth 800 tomans.

Currently, over 50 percent of the country's population is under age twenty. This population "bomb" is more threatening to hard-liners in power than is any foreign threat. These youth, along with the women of Iran, elected President Khatami and moderate reformist parliamentary members. They want an aggressive president who will stand for the rule of law. They want to see the government becoming more democratic and less theocratic. A country with such a vast natural and human resources, if managed well, can become one of the world's most prosperous nations.

In the age of globalization, Iranians do not feel as isolated as they once did. Now satellites and the Internet have reached even remote areas of the country. Thanks to Khatami's reforms, Internet cafes are all over larger Iranian cities. Due to improved communications, Iranians can easily contact their three million relatives who live abroad. Many of the one million Iranians who live in the United States regularly visit Iran, or are in touch via telephone, computer, or satellite TV. In fact, several Iranian TV stations broadcast from the United States and are viewed by Iranians inside Iran. Similarly, Iranians in the United States are able to watch Iranian TV broadcasts. Many Iranian children living in American cities are learning to speak Farsi by watching children's programs televised from Tehran.

In this age of information and connectivity, Iranians feel their concerns are being heard and seen by the rest of the world. To prove that they belong to the world community of nations and to demonstrate that they do not stand for terrorism and lawlessness, many young Iranians held a candlelight vigil in the streets of Tehran for the victims of the September 11, 2001, terrorist attacks in the United States. These young Iranians identify with a compassionate and caring Iran—a country that produced great scientists, philosophers, and poets like Sadi, whose words still resonate whenever one speaks of a united humanity. In the thirteenth century, Sadi wrote:

> *The children of Adam are limbs of each other*
> *Having been created of one essence.*
> *When the calamity of time afflicts one limb*
> *The other limbs cannot remain at rest.*
> *If thou hast no sympathy for the troubles of others*
> *Thou art unworthy to be called by the name of a man.*

Facts at a Glance

Land and People

Official Name	Islamic Republic of Iran
Location	Middle East; Southwest Asia; shares borders with Pakistan, Afghanistan, Turkmenistan, Azerbaijan, Armenia, Turkey, and Iraq
Area	636,296 square miles, three times the size of France
Climate	Diverse; mostly arid or semiarid, subtropical along Caspian Sea coast
Major Rivers	Karun, Dez, Karkheh, Sefidrud, Haraz
Major Mountains	Elburz Mountains (Damavand Summit: 18,606 feet), Zagros Mountains
Natural Hazards	Periodic droughts, floods; dust storms, sandstorms; earthquakes
Environmental Problems	Air pollution from vehicle emissions, refinery operations, and industrial effluents; deforestation; overgrazing; desertification
Population	70 million (2002 estimate); 62 percent living in cities
Natural Increase	1.2 percent (births: 18 per 1000; deaths: 6 per 1000, both for year 2001)
Capital	Tehran (7 million population)
Cities (1,000,000+)	Mashhad, Esfahan, Tabriz, Shiraz
Ethnic Groups	Persian (51 percent), Azerbaijani (24 percent), Gilaki and Mazandarani (8 percent), Kurd (7 percent), Arab (3 percent), Lur (2 percent), Baloch (2 percent), Turkoman (2 percent), others (1 percent)
Religions	Shiite Muslim, 89 percent; Sunni Muslim, 10 percent; Zoroastrians, Jews, Christians, Bahais, 1 percent
Languages	Official language: Farsi (Persian); other languages: Kurdish, Turkish, Arabic, Lori, Gilaki, Mazandarani, Balochi
Literacy Rate	78 percent
Average Life Expectancy	70 years (male 69, female 71)
National Holiday	Islamic Republic Day, April 1 (1979)

Government

Form of Government	Theocratic Islamic Republic
Government Branches	Executive, Judicial, Legislative
Head of State	Ayatollah Seyyed Ali Khamenei, the Supreme Religious Leader
President	Hojattolislam Mohammad Khatami
Constitution	December 3, 1979 (major revisions, 1989)
Suffrage	At age 15; Iranian citizenship required

Economy

Natural Resources	Petroleum, natural gas, copper, coal, chromium, iron zinc, lead, sulfur, manganese
Land Use	Arable land: 10 percent; permanent crops: 1 percent; permanent pastures: 27 percent; forests and woodland: 10 percent; other: 52 percent
Gross National Product	238,554 million US$ (1999)
Per Capita GDP	3,802 US$ (1999)
Share of Sectors for GDP	20.0 percent agriculture, 37.0 percent industry, 43.0 percent services (1999)
Agricultural Products	Wheat, rice, other grains, sugar, beets, fruits, nuts, cotton, dairy products, wool, caviar
Industries	Petroleum, petrochemicals, textiles, cement and other building materials, food processing (particularly sugar refining and vegetable oil production), metal fabricating
Major Imports	Total $15 billion (year 2000): machinery, metal works, foodstuffs, pharmaceutical, technical services, chemical products, military supplies
Major Exports	Total $25 billion (year 2000): petroleum, carpets, fruits, dried fruits (pistachio, raisin, date), caviar, petrochemicals, textiles, garments, agricultural products, iron and steel
Major Trading Partners	Japan, Germany, Italy, UAE, India, Turkey, China, Russia
Currency	Rial; Toman (10 Iranian Rials = 1 Toman); $1 = 800 Tomans (2002)

History at a Glance

3900 B.C.	Sialk (near Kashan), the first city on the Iranian Plateau, is built.
1500–800 B.C.	Persians and the Medes, two Aryan groups, enter Iranian Plateau.
1000 B.C.	Prophet Zoroaster introduces concepts of monotheism, duality of good and evil, angels, and heaven and hell.
559–530 B.C.	Achaemenid Empire: Cyrus the Great establishes the Persian Empire in 550 B.C.
334 B.C.	Alexander the Great invades Iran and burns the city of Persepolis.
323–141 B.C.	Seleucid Dynasty is established by one of Alexander's generals.
247 B.C. – 224 A.D.	Parthians defeat Greek Seleucids and rule over all of Persia
224–642 A.D.	Sassanids Empire: Ardeshir I begins the dynasty.
642	Iran falls to Arab Islamic army.
661–750	Umayyad Caliphate rule; Iran is ruled by Arabs.
750–1258	Abbasid Caliphate; adopts Sassanid administration systems, establishes extensive bureaucracy, hires Persian viziers.
820–1220	The Golden Age of Iranian and Islamic scientists and philosophers.
1220	Genghis Khan and his Mongol hordes attack Iran.
1405	Timur (Tamerlane), a Turco-Mongol leader, conquers Iran.
1501–1524	Safavid Dynasty: Shah Ismail I unites all of Persia under Iranian leadership.
1587–1629	Reign of Shah Abbas the Great marks the pinnacle of the Safavid dynasty.
1722	Mahmoud Afghan attacks Iran and captures Esfahan, ending the Safavids rule.
1729–1747	Nader Shah expels the Afghans and reunites the country.
1747–1779	Karim Khan Zand gains control of Iran; he rejects being called Shah or king.

1795–1925	Qajar Dynasty: Qajars succeed in reuniting the country.
1813; 1828	Qajars lose the Caucasus (present-day Georgia, Armenia, and Azerbaijan) to the Russians in two separate treaties: the Gulistan in 1813 and the Turkmanchay in1828.
1851–1906	Qajars lose central Asian provinces to the Russians and are forced to give up all claims on Afghanistan to the British.
1906	Constitutional Movement and establishment of Iran's first parliament or Majles; the beginning modern Iranian history.
1921	Reza Khan, an officer in the army, stages a coup against the last king of Qajar.
1925–1979	Pahlavi Dynasty: Reza Shah strengthens the authority of the central government.
1941	Reza Shah abdicates in favor of his son and is deported to Johannesburg; Mohammad Reza Shah becomes the new king.
1951–1953	Musaddeq Era: nationalization of Iranian oil; Shah leaves; CIA-supported coup brings Shah back to power.
1962–1963	Shah introduces his White Revolution (land reform, workers' rights, and women's suffrage, among other initiatives).
1963–1973	Iran enjoys economic growth, prosperity, and political stability. Arab oil embargo quadruples Iran's oil revenues to $20 billion a year; more money brings more corruption and inequality, which leads to Shah's fall.
1979	*January 20:* Ayatollah Khomeini returns to Iran after 14 years of exile.
	April: Islamic Republic of Iran is proclaimed following a national referendum.
	November 4: Student militants attack American embassy, taking Americans hostage.

1980   *January 12:* Bani Sadr is elected as the first president of the
        Islamic Republic.

        September 22: Iraqi army invades Iran to annex Shat al-Arab.

        September 22: American hostages are released.

1988   *July 3:* 290 passengers of an Iran Airbus airliner are shot down
        by the USS *Vincennes*.

        July 20, After 8 years of bloody war, Iran accepts the cease-fire
        with Iraq.

1989   *Feb. 14,* Ayatollah Khomeini issues a religious edict
        for assassination of Salman Rushdie, the author of
        The Satanic Verses.

        June 3, Ayatollah Khomeini dies.

        June 4: Ayatollah Khamenei becomes the new Supreme Leader.

        Aug. 17: Rafsanjani becomes president.

1990   *June 21:* A major earthquake kills 40,000 people.

        September 11: Iran and Iraq resume diplomatic relations.

1995   U.S. imposes oil and trade sanctions against Iran.

1997   *May 23:* Khatami is elected by 70 percent of the vote as
        new president.

1999   *July:* Prodemocracy students' demonstrations turns bloody
        when government guards attack demonstrators.

2000   *February 18:* Liberals and supporters of Khatami win 170 of
        the 290 seats in the parliamentary elections.

2000   *April 23:* Judiciary bans 16 reformist newspapers.

2001   *April:* Iran and Saudi Arabia sign major security accord to
        combat terrorism, drug trafficking, and organized crime.

2001   *June 8:* President Khatami is reelected for a second term
        with 77 percent of the vote.

2002   *January:* U.S. president Bush describes Iraq, Iran, and
        North Korea as an "axis of evil."

Books

Colbert Held, *Middle East Patterns: Places, Peoples, and Politics*, Third Edition, Westview Press, 2000

Masoud Kheirabadi, *Iranian Cities: Formation and Development*, Syracuse University Press, 2000

Arthur Upham Pope, *A Survey of Persian Art. 6 vols*, Oxford University Press, 1938-39.

Elaine Sciolino, *Persian Mirrors: the Elusive Face of Iran*, the Free Press, 2000

Websites

Statistical Center of Iran
http://www.unescap.org/pop/popin/profiles/iran/popin2.htm

Statistical, economic and social research and training center for Islamic countries
http://www.sesrtcic.org/defaulteng.shtml

Mage Publishers Inc.
http://www.mage.com/TLbody.html

The National Iranian American Council
http://cyberiran.com/history/

Columbia Encyclopedia
http://www.bartleby.com/65/ir/Iran.html

Amnesty International
http://www.bartleby.com/65/ir/Iran.html

Islamic Republic of Iran
http://www.mideastinfo.com/iran.htm

Country Analysis Brief
http://www.mideastinfo.com/iran.htm

"Recent Changes and Future of Fertility in Iran" by Mohammad Jalal Abbasi Shavazi
http://www.un.org/esa/population/publications/completingfertility/ABBASIpaper.PDF

Further Reading

A. J. Arberry, *The Legacy of Persia*, Oxford University Press, 1953.

Said Amir Arjomand, *The Turban for the Crown: The Islamic Revolution in Iran*, Oxford University Press, 1988.

Wilfried Buchta, *Who Rules Iran? : The Structure of Power in the Islamic Republic*, Washington Institute for Near East Policy, 2001.

Richard Cottam, *Iran and the United States: A Cold War Case Study*, University of Pittsburgh Press, 1988.

Hamid Dabashi, *Iranian Cinema: Past, Present, and Future*, Verso Books,

John Esposito, *Islam: The Straight Path*, Oxford University Press, 1991.

Grant Farr, *Modern Iran*, McGraw-Hill, 1999.

James Goode, *The United States and Iran: In the Shadow of Musaddiq*, St. Martin's Press, 1997.

Ahmad Karimi Hakkak, *Recasting Persian Poetry: Scenarios of Poetic Modernity in Iran*, University of Utah Press, 1995.

Michael Hillman, *Iranian Culture: A Persianist View*, University Press of America, 1990.

Farzaneh Milani, *Veils and Words*, Syracuse University Press, 1992.

Terrence O'Donnel, *Garden of the Brave in War: Reflections of Iran*, University of Chicago Press, 1980.

Shahrnush Parsipur, *Women Without Men*, Syracuse University Press, 1998.

I. P. Petrushevsky, *Islam in Iran*, translated by Hubert Evans, State University of New York, 1985.

Gary Sick, *All Fall Down: America's Tragic Encounter with Iran*, Penguin Books, 1986.

Soraya Sullivan, *Stories by Iranian Women Since the Revolution*, University of Texas Press, 1990.

Robin Wright, *The Last Great Revolution: Turmoil and Transformation in Iran*, Vintage Books, 2001.

Index

Index

page:

8:	Corbis	66:	New Millennium Images
11:	21st Century Publishing	71:	Afshin Valinejad/AP/Wide World Photos
14:	Corbis	72:	Campion/AP/Wide World Photos
19:	21st Century Publishing	83:	Ron Edmonds/AP/Wide World Photos
24:	New Millennium Images	86:	New Millennium Images
26:	New Millennium Images	93:	New Millennium Images
32:	Paul Almasy/Corbis	97:	New Millennium Images
37:	Roger Wood/Corbis	98:	New Millennium Images
40:	Kamran Jebreili/AP/Wide World Photos	102:	Kamran Jebreili/AP/Wide World Photos
47:	Bettmann/Corbis	107:	Hasan Sarbakhshian/AP/
50:	AP/Wide World Photos		Wide World Photos
56:	Hasan Sarbakhshian/AP/	114:	Hasan Sarbakhshian/AP/
	Wide World Photos		Wide World Photos
59:	Jerome Delay/AP/Wide World Photos	116:	Enric Marti/AP/Wide World Photos

Cover: Roger Wood/CORBIS

About the Author

MASOUD KHEIRABADI is an Iranian American who immigrated to the United States in 1976. He lived three years in Texas where he received his M.S. in agricultural mechanization from Texas A & I University (which later joined with Texas A & M). In 1979, he moved to Eugene, Oregon, and studied at the University of Oregon, where he received his M.A. and later Ph.D. in geography. He has taught at the University of Oregon, Lewis and Clark College, and Maryhurst University. He is currently teaching for the International Studies Program at Portland State University.

Professor Kheirabadi's research interest focuses on issues and problems of development in less-developed countries, with a regional emphasis on the Middle East. He is interested in issues concerning resource management, sustainable development, urbanization, population, race and ethnic relations, and cultural geography. Dr. Kheirabadi has published several books and articles on Middle Eastern issues. A third edition of his book *Iranian Cities* was recently published by the Syracuse University Press.

CHARLES F. ("FRITZ") GRITZNER is Distinguished Professor of Geography at South Dakota University in Brookings. He is now in his fifth decade of college teaching and research. During his career, he has taught more than 60 different courses, spanning the fields of physical, cultural, and regional geography. In addition to his teaching, he enjoys writing, working with teachers, and sharing his love for geography with students. As consulting editor for the MODERN WORLD NATIONS series, he has a wonderful opportunity to combine each of these "hobbies." Fritz has served as both president and executive director of the National Council for Geographic Education and has received the Council's highest honor, the George J. Miller Award for Distinguished Service.